Manifesting

A BEGINNER'S GUIDE

NICOLE WEISS

Leaping Hare Press

Quarto

First published in 2025 by Leaping Hare Press,
an imprint of The Quarto Group.
One Triptych Place, London, SE1 9SH,
United Kingdom
T (0)20 7700 9000
www.Quarto.com

EEA Representation, WTS Tax d.o.o., Žanova ulica 3, 4000 Kranj, Slovenia

Text copyright © 2025 Nicole Weiss
Illustrations copyright © 2025 Annie Tarasova
Design copyright © 2025 Quarto Publishing Plc

Nicole Weiss and Annie Tarasova have asserted their moral right to be identified as the Author and Illustrator respectively of this Work in accordance with the Copyright Designs and Patents Act 1988.

All rights reserved. No part of this book may be reproduced or utilised in any form or by any means, electronic or mechanical, including photocopying, recording or by any information storage and retrieval system, without permission in writing from Leaping Hare Press.

Every effort has been made to trace the copyright holders of material quoted in this book.
If application is made in writing to the publisher, any omissions will be included in future editions.

A catalog record for this book is available from the British Library.

ISBN 978-1-8360-0579-7
Ebook ISBN 978-1-8360-0580-3

10 9 8 7 6 5 4 3 2 1

Design by Francesca Corsini

Editorial Director: Monica Perdoni
Project Editor: Chloe Murphy
Editor: Katerina Menhennet
Senior Designer: Renata Latipova
Production Controller: Rohana Yusof

Printed in China

Contents

Introduction — 6
My Story — 8
How to Use This Book — 10
Embark on Your Manifestation Journey — 12

Step 1 | UNVEIL YOUR WISHES — 18

Dig Up Your Dreams Journaling Exercise — 24
Create Your Wish List — 26
Your Dream Life Vision Board — 32
Design Your Dream Day — 34
Embrace Your True Self — 38

Step 2 | BREAK FREE FROM SELF-DOUBT — 40

Face Your Self-Doubt Exercise — 46
Challenge Your Inner Critic Exercise — 48
Positive Mindset Affirmation Ritual — 50
Meditation to Clear Mental Clutter — 52
Ritual for Letting Go — 54
Discover Your Power — 58

Step 3 | FIND YOUR INNER POWER   60

The Law Of Attraction   66
The Law Of Assumption   68
Align with Your Authentic Self Visualization   70
Find Your True North Exercise   72
Guided Meditation to Meet Your Future Self   74
Mirror, Mirror Self-Love Ritual   76
Shower Ritual to Manifest Your Dreams   78
Believe It, Receive It   82

Step 4 TAKE INSPIRED ACTION   84

Create Your Manifestation Road Map   90
Intuition Check-In   96
The Inspired Action Dare   98
The Inspired Action Reward System   100
The "Universe, Show Me a Sign" Challenge   102
The Cosmic Scavenger Hunt   104
The Dream Decoder   106
Making Your Dreams Happen   110

Step 5 TRUST THE UNIVERSE   112

The Law of Detachment   118
The Fertile Ground of Gratitude   120
Release and Flow Water Ritual   122
Release Attachment Meditation   124
Burning Bowl Release Ritual   126
Short Daily Gratitude Practice   128
Gratitude Jar for Abundance   130
Gratitude Letter to the Universe   132
Embracing the Magic of the Universe   136

Manifesting by Purpose — 138

MANIFEST LOVE AND SELF-LOVE — 142
The Love Letter Method — 144
The Whisper Method — 145
Future Love Time Capsule Manifestation — 146
The Self-Love Date Ritual — 148
The Mirror Work for Love Method — 149

MANIFEST MONEY AND ABUNDANCE — 152
The 369 Money Manifesting Exercise — 154
The Abundance Check Exercise — 156
The Money Magnet Meditation — 158
The Decluttering Method — 160

MANIFEST CAREER SUCCESS — 164
The Talk Show Exercise — 166
The Act As If Method — 168
Living the Dream Journal — 170

MANIFEST HEALTH AND WELLNESS — 174
The Healthy Habits Ritual — 176
The Body Gratitude Ritual — 178
The Recipe Adventure — 180
The Mindful Grocery Shopping Exercise — 181

MANIFEST PURPOSE AND FULFILLMENT — 184
The Soul's Calling Journaling Exercise — 186
The Purposeful Playlist Creation — 188
The Inner Child Reconnection — 189
The Purposeful Pause Meditation — 190

MANIFEST CONFIDENCE AND SELF-ESTEEM — 194
The Inner Champion Affirmation Mirror Ritual — 196
The Celebrate Your Wins Exercise — 197
The Confidence-Boosting Visualization — 198

MANIFEST SPIRITUAL GROWTH — 202
The Soul-Nourishing Activities List — 204
The Sacred Space Creation — 205
The Spiritual Exploration Adventure — 206
The Sacred Sound Bath Experience — 207

MANIFEST INNER PEACE AND HAPPINESS — 210
The Inner Child Playdate — 212
The Acts of Kindness Challenge — 213
The Inner Oasis Visualization — 214

Conclusion — 218
About the Author — 220
About the Illustrator — 220
Recommended Reading — 221
Index — 222
Acknowledgments — 224

Introduction

Man·i·fest·ing

The act of making something happen by imagining it and consciously believing that it will happen.

Deep down, you know there's more to life than the daily grind. You crave a life filled with purpose, passion, and the exhilarating feeling of achieving your wildest dreams. Maybe it's a career that ignites your soul, a love story that sweeps you off your feet, or the freedom to travel the world. These desires aren't foolish fantasies; they're whispers from your authentic self, urging you to break free from limitations and step into a life that feels extraordinary.

But the path to your dreams can feel shrouded in mystery. You may see others effortlessly attract success and abundance, while your own attempts fizzle out, leaving you feeling frustrated and powerless. The truth is, they've tapped into a powerful force within themselves: the ability to manifest their desires.

This book isn't a collection of empty promises or quick fixes. Manifesting is a journey of self-discovery and a process of aligning your thoughts, intentions, and actions with the abundant energy of the universe. It's about shedding limiting beliefs that hold you back, developing unwavering trust in your own power, and taking inspired action to bridge the gap between where you are and where you desire to be.

Within these pages, you'll embark on a transformative adventure. We'll explore practical tools and techniques to unlock the magic within. You'll learn to harness the power of visualization, cultivate an attitude of gratitude, and quiet the inner critic that whispers doubt. Most importantly, you'll discover the profound truth: you are not a passive observer in the face of your dreams; you are the co-creator of your reality.

My Story

Have you ever had one of those moments where you stumble upon something that completely changes the course of your life? That happened to me years ago in a dusty old bookstore, and it set me on a path of incredible transformation.

Picture this: New York City, pouring rain, and me, wandering aimlessly into a used bookstore. I'm browsing the shelves when I spot a beat-up old book called *The Power of Intention*, tucked away in a corner, almost like it's waiting for me. Curiosity piqued, I grab it and start reading. At first, it all sounds a little out there. But as I delve deeper, I start to see the world through a different lens, realizing that we have much more influence over our reality than we're led to believe. It's like a switch flips in my brain, and I'm ready to put this manifestation thing to the test.

Fast-forward a few years, and I'm living proof that this stuff works. I've manifested a dream collaboration with a renowned artist, traveled to exotic destinations I'd only seen in pictures, and even achieved the financial freedom to pursue my passions fulltime. It wasn't always easy, but with each success, my belief in the power of manifestation grew stronger.

But it's not just about the flashy results. It's about the countless hours I've spent studying, experimenting, and refining my techniques. I've learned to tap into my intuition, set clear intentions, and visualize my desires with unwavering focus. I've mastered the art of letting go and trusting in the universe to deliver. And most importantly, I've learned to embrace the journey, with all its twists and turns.

I've now become a guide for others seeking to manifest their own dreams. I've coached countless individuals, helping them break through limiting beliefs and step into their power.

I've seen firsthand the incredible transformations that can happen when you align your thoughts, feelings, and actions with your deepest desires.

So, if you're ready to embark on your own manifestation adventure, I'm here to show you the way.

How to Use This Book

Think of this book as your trusty sidekick on your manifestation journey. It's not just about reading the words; it's about diving in and applying these ideas to your own life.

The five steps in this book are your road map to manifesting your dreams. They're designed to flow seamlessly, each step building on the last. But here's the cool part: you set the pace.

Some steps might naturally take more time, and that's okay. It's all about honoring your own unique journey. These steps are here to empower you and help you create a life that lights you up.

Come back to them whenever you need a boost, a reminder, or a fresh perspective. Here's how to get the most out this book:

KEEP A MANIFESTATION JOURNAL
I recommend acquiring a fresh journal or notebook that you can use to practice just the exercises in this book in. This will help you track your journey and progress and keep everything together in one place.

COME WITH AN OPEN MIND
Be curious and willing to explore new ideas. Forget any preconceived notions about manifestation and just see where this book takes you.

TAKE IT SLOW
Don't try to speed-read your way to enlightenment. Take your time with each chapter. Let the ideas sink in, and maybe jot down some notes or highlight parts that speak to you. Come back to sections whenever you need a refresher.

GET YOUR HANDS DIRTY
Manifestation is like any other skill: you've got to practice. Try out the exercises and techniques in this book and stick with it, even if you don't see results right away.

BE KIND TO YOURSELF
Transformation takes time. Don't beat yourself up if things don't change overnight. Celebrate every little win, and remember, you're on your own unique path. You may even like to connect with other people who are also exploring manifestation, as it's always more fun to share the journey with others.

CREATE YOUR VIBE
Find a cozy spot where you can focus and really connect with the book. Light a candle, put on some chill music, and set the mood.

TRUST THE PROCESS
Believe in the power of the universe and know it has your back. Let go of any doubts or worries, and just enjoy the ride.

Embark on Your Manifestation Journey

"Manifesting" is a word that's often shrouded in a veil of mysticism and wishful thinking, but beneath the surface, there's a profound truth waiting to be discovered. Manifestation is about understanding that you're not just a passive observer in the grand scheme of things, but an active participant, capable of shaping your reality through your thoughts, beliefs, and actions.

This book is your invitation to harness that power, to become a conscious creator of your own life. It's not about wishful thinking or magical spells; it's about understanding the mechanics of the mind, the energy of the universe, and how you can align them to manifest your dreams.

In this book, you'll discover a treasure trove of manifestation techniques, from mindset shifts to self-love rituals to powerful universe alignment strategies. Whether you crave a soul-stirring love story, a career that ignites your passion, or a life overflowing with abundance, this book equips you with the tools to make it happen.

Step 1

UNVEIL YOUR WISHES

Imagine your heart as a treasure chest filled with hidden desires. This step is about unlocking that chest and discovering the jewels within. It's a journey of self-discovery that invites you to explore the depths of your soul. Let go of limitations and expectations, and allow your imagination to run wild. Once you've unearthed these desires, you'll transform them into a powerful wish list, which will become a guiding star on your manifestation journey.

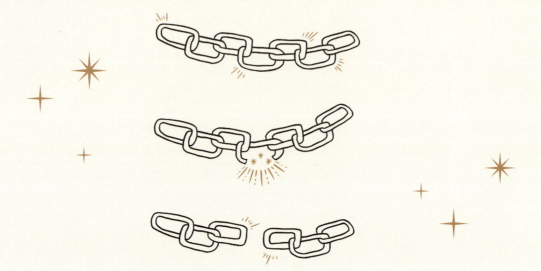

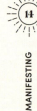

Step 2

BREAK FREE FROM SELF-DOUBT

Self-doubt can be like a harsh critic, whispering negativity and undermining your confidence. In this step, you'll learn to silence that inner critic and replace self-limiting beliefs with empowering affirmations. Think of this step as clearing the canvas, preparing it for the vibrant colors of your dreams.

Step 3

FIND YOUR INNER POWER

This step is about tapping into your inner power and understanding the core principles of the Law of Attraction, a guiding force that shapes our reality. This is where the true magic begins. You'll learn to harness the power of your mind through visualization, creating mental images so vivid they feel almost tangible, and you'll explore exercises that prepare you to take the next big steps on your manifestation journey.

Step 4

TAKE INSPIRED ACTION

This crucial step is all about taking action and harmonizing your actions with the natural flow of the universe. In it, you'll learn to recognize signs from the universe, follow your intuition, and take crucial steps that move you closer to your goals. It's about dancing with the universe, and co-creating a life that feels both magical and aligned.

Step 5

TRUST THE UNIVERSE

Just as a painter steps back to allow the masterpiece to reveal itself, so too must you learn to trust the process of manifestation. In this final step, you'll learn to cultivate patience and gratitude as you witness your desires taking shape, releasing control and allowing them to unfold in perfect timing.

Unveil YOUR Wishes

Rewrite YOUR Story

Every adventure needs a destination in mind and road map to guide you there. Likewise, manifesting your dreams requires a clear idea of where you want to go and a plan for getting there. In this chapter, you'll embark on a journey of introspection to uncover your goals and wishes. You'll being to visualize your manifestation destination, ready to set sail.

Unveiling Your Wishes

The first step on your journey is to uncover your wishes, which will act as the foundation you'll build everything else on. This isn't just about making a list of things you want. It's about digging deep and connecting with the truest desires of your heart. What makes your spirit soar? What dreams keep you up at night, filled with excitement? These are the questions that lead you to your authentic desires.

This is an inner journey of peeling back the layers and discovering what truly matters to you. Your desires are like a unique fingerprint, a guide toward your full potential. Your desires also aren't set in stone, and can change and grow as you do. Embrace that flexibility, allowing your wishes to evolve.

By clearly defining your desires, you're not just making a mental checklist; you're creating a powerful blueprint for your future. As you begin to explore your desires in this chapter, pay close attention to how they make you feel. Does a particular wish fill you with excitement, passion, or a deep sense of peace? These emotions are signs that you're on the right track, aligned with your authentic self.

When a desire truly energizes you, that's where the magic of manifestation starts to spark.

UNVEILING YOUR WISHES

Imagine gazing into a crystal ball, not to foresee the future, but to unveil your wishes. Like shimmering jewels within, your desires reveal the true essence of your soul. Uncovering them is like polishing the crystal, allowing its inner radiance to shine through. It's about delving deep within to understand what excites you and makes your heart sing.

By aligning your actions with these authentic wishes, you're not only setting goals but also creating a life that feels aligned with who you are. You are the architect of your destiny, and your desires are the precious stones you build it with.

Your desires, like living things, will naturally evolve and shift as you grow. Embrace this flexibility, allowing your vision to shift and expand. By clearly defining your desires, you're paving the way for a life that truly resonates with your soul.

DIG UP YOUR DREAMS JOURNALING EXERCISE

This first exercise on your manifestation journey will help you to begin uncovering your manifestation desires. Let your imagination run wild as you explore them, and don't hold back—write down everything that comes to mind. Remember, this is a personal journey, so be honest with yourself.

You will need your journal and a pen for this exercise.

1| Find somewhere you can sit comfortably and undisturbed. When you're ready to begin, take a few deep breaths.

2| Open your journal to a new page, close your eyes, and forget about what everyone else expects of you. Ask yourself: What truly sets my soul on fire? What makes my heart sing? Is it the thrill of creating something beautiful, the satisfaction of helping others, or the joy of learning something new every day? Don't be afraid to dream big and be specific.

3| Write down your answers to these questions, taking your time to think about your answers.

4| Reflect upon your answers and any initial dreams and goals they reveal to you.

5| If you already have some dreams in mind, picture yourself achieving your biggest one, and write down how it makes you feel. The feeling is key, as feelings are like a compass, helping you understand what you truly desire.

Tips for Uncovering Your Dreams

It's completely normal to feel unsure about what to manifest. Sometimes, our desires are hidden beneath layers of self-doubt or societal expectations, so don't worry if you're not immediately flooded with ideas. Discovery is part of the journey. Here are some additional journaling prompts to help you uncover your heart's true desires:

REFLECT ON YOUR CHILDHOOD

What did you dream of becoming? What brought you joy as a child?

IDENTIFY YOUR STRENGTHS

What are you naturally good at? How can you leverage your talents?

CHALLENGE YOUR LIMITATIONS

What would you do if fear didn't exist?

LOOK AT YOUR ROLE MODELS

What qualities do you admire in others? How can you incorporate those into your life?

CONSIDER YOUR VALUES

What is truly important to you? How can your desires align with your values?

CREATE YOUR WISH LIST

Your dreams are unique to you, and it's time to give them a voice. Let's translate your dreams so far into a powerful wish list: a heartfelt declaration to the universe about what truly makes your soul sing.

Your wish list isn't just a checklist of things to acquire; it's a chance to step into your power and claim the life you deserve. Your wish list is also a living document, so don't be afraid to take your time with this exercise and to change and update your list as you progress along your manifestation path.

You will need your journal and a pen for this exercise.

1| Find a calm and peaceful environment where you won't be interrupted.

2| Write down your desires, jotting down everything that comes to mind, no matter how big or small. Don't overthink it. Just let your thoughts flow freely. Let go of any doubts or limitations.

3| Once you have an initial list, start to refine your desires. Instead of "I want a new car," write, "I have a sleek, red convertible." Use positive language and focus on what you do want, not what you don't want. For example, instead of "I don't want to be broke," write, "Financial abundance."

4| As you write, imagine yourself already having what you desire. Feel the emotions associated with it, and listen to your inner guidance. Some desires might surprise you.

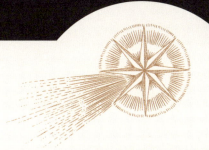

Tips for Making Your Wish List Magical

As you create your wish list, remember that it's not just about the things you want to manifest; it's also about the person you want to become. What kind of person do you aspire to be? How do you want to contribute to your community and the world around you? What legacy do you want to leave behind?

BE SPECIFIC

The clearer your wishes are, the clearer the message you send to the universe. Instead of wishing for more money, write something more specific, like "Enough money to comfortably travel to Europe next year."

DREAM BIG, BUT START SMALL

Include a mix of big, audacious wishes and smaller, more achievable ones. This helps you build momentum and confidence as you start manifesting those smaller wins.

FOCUS ON THE JOURNEY TOO

Instead of just wishing for the end result, include wishes that focus on the process. For example, "Dedicate 30 minutes every day to painting."

Struggling to Find Your Goals?

If you're still struggling to define or refine your wish list, the following pages include some example wish lists to help inspire you.

ARTIST'S WISH LIST

CREATIVE FULFILLMENT

✦ Create a body of work that resonates deeply with others
✦ Have my art featured in a solo exhibition at a prestigious gallery
✦ Build a strong and supportive community of fellow artists
✦ Develop a unique artistic style that is recognized and admired

FINANCIAL STABILITY

✦ Earn a sustainable income from my art
✦ Secure grants or sponsorships to support my creative endeavors
✦ Sell my artwork consistently to collectors

PERSONAL GROWTH

✦ Overcome creative blocks and build a consistent artistic practice
✦ Build confidence in my artistic abilities
✦ Develop strong time management and organizational skills
✦ Expand my knowledge of art history and theory

LIFESTYLE

✦ Live in a creative and inspiring space
✦ Travel to art museums and cultural centers for inspiration
✦ Have the freedom to dedicate ample time to my art

STAY-AT-HOME PARENT'S WISH LIST

FAMILY AND HOME

- ✦ A harmonious and loving family environment
- ✦ Healthy, happy, and thriving children
- ✦ A beautiful and organized home that is a sanctuary for the family
- ✦ Sufficient financial support for family needs

PERSONAL GROWTH

- ✦ Joy and fulfillment in the role of a stay-at-home parent
- ✦ Lots of patience and resilience
- ✦ Plenty of hobbies and interests
- ✦ Strong friendships and connections

HEALTH AND WELLNESS

- ✦ Sufficient energy and vitality to keep up with family life
- ✦ Regular opportunities for exercise and self-care
- ✦ A balanced and nutritious diet for the whole family
- ✦ Sufficient sleep and rest

FUTURE GOALS

- ✦ Opportunities for personal and professional growth
- ✦ Financial security for the family's future
- ✦ Memorable family vacations and adventures
- ✦ Contributing positively to the community

PROFESSIONAL ATHLETE'S WISH LIST

PERFORMANCE AND CAREER

- Achieve peak physical condition and optimal athletic performance
- Win [specific championship or award]
- Become a role model and inspire others
- Secure lucrative endorsement deals

FINANCIAL SUCCESS

- Build a substantial net worth through endorsements and investments
- Create multiple streams of income beyond athletic careers
- Achieve financial security for myself and my family

PERSONAL GROWTH

- Develop strong mental resilience and focus
- Nurture leadership qualities and inspire teammates
- Build a strong support network of family and friends
- Pursue interests and hobbies outside of sports

LIFESTYLE

- Live in a luxurious and comfortable home
- Travel to exotic destinations and experience different cultures
- Give back to the community through charitable endeavors

SPIRITUAL SEEKER'S WISH LIST

INNER PEACE AND CONNECTION

✦ Cultivate a deep sense of inner peace and contentment
✦ Establish a strong connection to my intuition and inner wisdom
✦ Find a spiritual community that supports and inspires me

EMOTIONAL WELL-BEING

✦ Heal past emotional wounds and traumas
✦ Develop emotional resilience and self-compassion
✦ Foster healthy and fulfilling relationships

PERSONAL GROWTH

✦ Embark on a journey of self-discovery and self-acceptance
✦ Release limiting beliefs and embrace my true potential
✦ Live authentically and align my actions with my values

PURPOSE AND CONTRIBUTION

✦ Discover my life's purpose and contribute to the world in a meaningful way
✦ Use my gifts and talents to serve others and make a positive impact
✦ Inspire and uplift those around me

LIFESTYLE

✦ Live in a peaceful and harmonious environment
✦ Spend time in nature and connect with its healing energy
✦ Dedicate time for meditation, prayer, or other spiritual practices
✦ Surround myself with people who support my spiritual growth

YOUR DREAM LIFE VISION BOARD

Now that you've started to develop an initial wish list for your manifestations, it's time to create a vision board for your dream life to begin sending your wishes out into the world.

A vision board is like a collage of your future self and a visual reminder of all the amazing things you're going to manifest. It's a fun and powerful way to keep your goals front and center, reminding your subconscious mind of what you're working toward.

You'll need a poster board, some old magazines, newspapers, colorful markers, scissors, and glue, or access to a computer, software, and printer to create a digital board.

1| Take some time to think about your goals and dreams. What do you want to achieve? What kind of life do you envision for yourself?

2| Flip through magazines and newspapers or browse online for images that represent your desires. It can be pictures of dream homes, beautiful places, happy people, or anything that visually captures your goals.

3| Arrange those images on your board in a way that feels good and inspires you. Add some motivational quotes, affirmations, or even your own drawings to make it extra personal.

4| If you're working digitally, print your board. Then, find a spot in your home or workspace where you'll see your vision board every day. This constant visual reminder will keep your dreams at the forefront of your mind and reinforce your manifestation intentions.

Tips for Creating Your Vision Board

You've dreamed big, gathered inspiring images, and arranged them in a way that speaks to your soul. Now it's time to take your vision board to the next level! Here are some tips to make it even more powerful and effective:

INFUSE IT WITH EMOTION

Don't just look at your vision board, feel it. As you place each image, visualize yourself living that reality. The stronger the emotions you connect to your board, the stronger its pull will be.

MAKE IT A RITUAL

Make the creation of your vision board a sacred experience. Light candles, play calming music, and set an intention for your dreams to manifest.

SET THE MOOD

What's the main feeling you want to capture? Fearless explorer? Zen master? Artistic soul? Having a theme helps you narrow your focus and gives your board a cohesive feel.

EMBRACE IMPERFECTION

Sometimes the most powerful boards are the ones that are a little messy and raw.

DESIGN YOUR DREAM DAY

To help you begin manifesting your dreams, this exercise invites you to fast-forward into your dream life and experience it today. It's like a dress rehearsal for your future self, allowing you to embody the energy of your desires and accelerate their manifestation, as well as check that they're right for you.

Activities to practice on your dream day could include creative pursuits, self-care rituals like a luxurious bath, practicing a new skill that supports your goals spending time in nature, connecting with loved ones, engaging in acts of service, taking a class, or reading a book.

You will need your journal and a pen for this exercise.

1| Find somewhere you can sit comfortably and undisturbed. When you're ready to begin, take a few deep breaths.

2| Open your journal to a new page and imagine you've already achieved your biggest goal. What does your ideal day look like? Write down what it looks like and take your time to identify the details, such as what your dream self is wearing, doing, and feeling.

3| Once you have an image in mind, create a schedule for your dream day. Fill your day with activities that reflect your dream life.

4| Schedule a day when you can practice your dream day, and try to follow it as closely as you can at this early stage of your journey.

5| At the end of your dream day, take some time to journal about your experience. What did you learn about yourself and your desires? Have any of them changed?

Tips for Designing Your Dream Day

As you imagine your dream day, visualize your future self in all their glory. How do they carry themselves each day? How do they interact with others? What habits have they cultivated? Here are some examples to help you design your dream day:

MORNING

Wake up in my beautiful writing space, overlooking a peaceful garden. Enjoy a healthy breakfast while reviewing my latest manuscript.

MIDMORNING

Head to a cozy coffee shop to write, surrounded by the buzz of creative energy.

AFTERNOON

Meet with my editor to discuss my upcoming book launch.

EVENING

Celebrate my success with a delicious dinner with friends, followed by a relaxing bath and reading before bed.

JOURNAL PROMPTS TO UNVEIL YOUR WISHES

1
What brings me the greatest joy and fulfillment?

2
If I could live without limitations, what would my life look like?

3
What kind of impact do I want to make on the world?

4
What am I truly passionate about?

5
What makes me feel most alive?

6
What do I secretly dream about but haven't allowed myself to fully consider?

7
What legacy do I want to leave behind?

8
How do I want to be remembered?

DAILY AFFIRMATIONS TO UNVEIL YOUR WISHES

I am confident in my ability to manifest my dreams.

I am open to receiving my heart's desires.

I am worthy of achieving my dreams.

I am aligned with my true purpose.

I attract abundance and joy into my life.

I am powerful and capable of manifesting my wishes.

I am deserving of all the happiness life has to offer.

Embrace Your True Self

To truly step into your power and become the best version of yourself, you first need to let go of the old you—the one shaped by expectations and outdated stories. Unveiling your wishes is a huge first step, as it's about peeling back those layers of external expectations and uncovering what lights you up.

By connecting with your authentic self and identifying the dreams that make your heart sing, you're setting off on a powerful journey of creation.

Now that you've begun to unveil your wishes and develop a deeper understanding of your desires, it's time to address the internal barriers that may be holding you back. Self-doubt, limiting beliefs, and fear can all sabotage your manifestation journey before it even begins.

This next section will guide you through techniques for identifying and overcoming these internal obstacles. We'll explore strategies for challenging negative self-talk, nurturing self-compassion, and building unshakable self-belief.

By addressing these inner obstacles, you'll create a strong foundation for success and pave the way for a more confident, empowered you. As you move

forward to the next step, remember that manifestation is a balance between setting intentions and going with the flow. Trust your gut and believe in the endless possibilities that are out there for you. This is just the beginning.

The next step is all about breaking free from the mold that no longer fits you and embracing the freedom to create a new definition for yourself. Sure, this might feel a bit scary at first, like stepping out of your comfort zone. But remember, growth doesn't happen when we stay stuck in the same old patterns.

Break FREE FROM Self-Doubt

It's time to clear some space for new growth, let go of any expectations and societal pressures that might be holding you back, and embrace the amazing person you're meant to be. When you ditch limiting beliefs and self-doubt, you open the door to endless possibilities. It might be a bit tough at first, but it's key to unlocking your full potential.

Breaking Free from Self-Doubt

A major obstacle you might face on this journey is the voice of self-doubt. Your inner critic may whisper negativity and discouragement, telling you things like, "You can't do it," "You're not good enough," or "What's the point?"

Self-doubt can be like a heavy weight holding you back from reaching your full potential, and it can show up in lots of sneaky ways, whether it's through the chatter of the inner critic, imposter syndrome, fear of failure, perfectionism, constantly measuring yourself against others, or feeling like you're never quite good enough.

Whichever form it takes, self-doubt is a common roadblock on the path to manifestation, and it is often deeply rooted in past experiences and messages we've received from the world around us.

Were you ever told you weren't good enough, smart enough, or talented enough? Did you feel pressure to be perfect, or were your mistakes met with harsh criticism? Perhaps you were compared to others, leaving you feeling inadequate. These experiences, big and small, can leave lasting imprints on our subconscious minds, shaping how we see ourselves and the world.

Take a moment to reflect on your childhood. Can you recall any specific instances where you may have internalized messages of self-doubt? Were there any recurring themes or patterns in your upbringing that might have contributed to these feelings? Understanding the origins of your self-doubt is like finding the source of a leak. Once you know where it's coming from, you can start to patch it up and prevent further damage.

When you figure out what's holding you back, like negative thoughts and doubts, you can start to change them. This might not be easy at first, but it's really important for reaching your full potential. Once you do this you'll have many more opportunities.

Remember, you are not defined by your past experiences. You have the power to rewrite your story, starting today.

FACE YOUR SELF-DOUBT EXERCISE

Have you started a project all fired up, only to have doubts creep in and leave you frozen? Or hesitated to chase a dream because a little voice inside says, "What if I mess up?" This is self-doubt in action.

To set the wheels in motion for working toward a goal, you first need to shine a light on your self-doubt and inner critic and replace it with a supportive voice. A key step in arming yourself against sneaky self-doubt is to figure out what triggers it.

In this exercise, you will learn how to identify, acknowledge, and reframe self-doubting thoughts that may be hindering your manifestations.

You will need your journal and a pen for this exercise.

1| Take a few moments to reflect on your manifestation goals and wish list. What doubtful thoughts or limiting beliefs arise when you think about achieving those goals? Write them down in your journal. For example, "I'm not good enough to achieve this."

2| Read through your list, then take a deep breath and acknowledge that these thoughts exist. It's okay to feel doubt; try to accept these thoughts without judgment or criticism.

3| Now, it's time to challenge those self-doubting thoughts and reframe them into empowering beliefs. For each negative thought, write down a positive affirmation or statement that counters it. For example, "I'm not good enough to achieve this" can become "I am capable and deserving of achieving my goals."

4| Read your positive affirmations aloud several times, allowing the words to sink in and resonate.

Tips for Facing Your Self-Doubt

By replacing negative self-talk with positive affirmations, you can start to rewire your brain. It takes time and practice, but the rewards are worth it. If you're finding it hard to communicate with and face your inner critic, the following tips may help:

BE HONEST WITH YOURSELF

Don't try to sugarcoat or dismiss your self-doubting thoughts. The more honest you are, the more effective this exercise will be.

BE KIND TO YOURSELF

Remember that self-doubt is normal. Don't beat yourself up for having these thoughts.

BE PATIENT

It takes time to reprogram your subconscious mind. Keep practicing this exercise and be patient with yourself.

LOOK AT YOUR ROLE MODELS

What qualities do you admire in others? How can you incorporate those into your life?

CELEBRATE YOUR PROGRESS

As you start to notice a shift in your mindset, take a moment to celebrate your progress. This will help you stay motivated.

CHALLENGE YOUR INNER CRITIC EXERCISE

Everyone struggles with self-doubt at times, and it can be tempting to beat yourself up over these doubts. Self-doubt is a tough opponent, but it's not unbeatable. By challenging limiting beliefs, you can build a mindset that's resilient and empowered.

This exercise invites you to engage in a direct and inquisitive dialogue with your self-doubt to uncover its origins, challenge it, and build a better relationship with it.

By practicing self-compassion here, you'll create a safe space for yourself to grow and learn, so try to treat yourself like you would treat your best friend as you work through this conversation.

You will need your journal and a pen for this exercise.

1| Begin your letter by talking directly to your self-doubt.

2| Write down any specific self-doubting thoughts that have been occurring lately. Be clear and detailed, like you're presenting evidence to a jury. For example, "You say things like, 'I'll never be able to afford my dream home' or 'I'm not smart enough to start my own business.'"

3| Now, it's time to turn the tables on those self-doubting thoughts. Question them, challenge them, and dig deep to figure out where they came from and whether they're even true. Then, rewrite them into statements that actually reflect your awesome potential. For example, replace "I'll never afford my dream home" with "I am open to attracting the financial resources for my dream home."

4| Conclude your letter with a firm declaration of your determination, like "I am capable, worthy, and deserving of my dreams."

Tips for Befriending Your Inner Critic

This exercise isn't about shutting down your inner critic entirely, but about changing the conversation. By having an open and honest chat with it, you're taking back control of your story and creating space for your dreams to come true. Here are some further ways to deepen the conversation:

DIG DEEP

The more you understand the origins of your self-doubt, the easier it will be to dismantle it.

LOOK FOR PROOF

Think about times in your life when you've proven those self-doubts wrong. Those moments are like gold, as they show you what you're truly capable of and can help you build unshakable confidence.

READ IT ALOUD

Give your words power by reading your letter aloud with conviction.

POSITIVE MINDSET AFFIRMATION RITUAL

Just like sunshine nourishes a garden, a positive mindset helps your dreams to grow. With a little care and attention, you can nurture an inner world filled with optimism and resilience. This exercise is all about cultivating those good vibes.

You will need your journal and a pen for this exercise.

1| Start by jotting down three to five things you're grateful for right now. It could be anything big or small, like the smell of your morning coffee, a supportive friend, or just the fact that you woke up today. Let those feelings of gratitude fill you up and set the mood.

2| Write down three to five positive affirmations about yourself, and keep them in the present tense, like they're already happening. For example, "I am worthy of love and abundance. I am crushing my goals and living my dreams."

3| Close your eyes and take a few deep breaths. Picture a warm, golden light glowing from your heart, spreading throughout your whole body. Feel the warmth and positivity washing over you, melting away any negativity or self doubt.

4| While you're basking in that inner sunshine, repeat your affirmations out loud. Say them like you mean it, letting those words sink deep into your mind and soul.

Tips for Nurturing Your Inner Sunshine

Having a positive outlook doesn't mean ignoring the hard stuff; it's about believing in your ability to overcome obstacles and find solutions. By nurturing a positive mindset, you're basically giving yourself a superpower: the ability to face life's challenges with courage and resilience. To get the most out of this exercise:

GET CREATIVE

You can do this exercise anywhere—on a walk, in the shower, or even while listening to your favorite playlist.

KEEP IT CONSISTENT

The more you practice, the easier it'll be to focus on the good stuff and build that positive mindset. Make this exercise a regular part of your routine. Start or end your day by soaking up some inner sunshine and reminding yourself how awesome you are.

Meditation to Clear Mental Clutter

Your brain is a lot like a supercomputer, constantly learning and adapting. It's got this amazing ability called neuroplasticity, which means you can rewire it for success, as when you challenge negative thought patterns, you create new pathways in your brain that support a more positive mindset. Alongside challenging self-doubting thoughts, learning how to let go of thoughts is an important part of this rewiring process.

Meditation is like a mental detox, clearing away negative thought patterns and making room for positivity and empowerment. This meditation will help you chill out and observe your thoughts without judgment, ready to let them drift away.

1| Find a quiet spot where you can relax without interruptions, and sit or lie down in a comfy position.

2| Gently close your eyes and take a few deep breaths. Inhale slowly through your nose, filling your lungs with air. Exhale slowly through your mouth, letting go of any tension. Keep breathing deeply and evenly throughout the meditation.

3| Now, observe your thoughts as they pop up. There's no need to control them or judge them, simply notice them coming and going. Think of each thought as a cloud drifting across the vast sky of your mind.

4| When negative thoughts occur, try to acknowledge them without getting caught up in them. Simply allow each cloud to float on by, gently releasing them into the mental atmosphere.

5 As you release those negative thoughts, focus on positive affirmations or images. Picture yourself crushing your goals, feeling confident and successful, and visualize your dreams becoming reality.

6 If your mind starts to wander (and it will), gently bring your attention back to your breath. Your breath is your anchor, keeping you grounded in the present moment.

7 Keep this practice going for 5-10 minutes and when you're ready to wrap up, slowly open your eyes and take a few moments to come back to the real world.

RITUAL FOR LETTING GO

This ritual is a powerful way to clear out old baggage and create space for new beginnings. It's about acknowledging what no longer serves you and choosing to let it go. The most important part of this ritual is the intention behind it. Focus on the feeling of release and the excitement about creating space for new possibilities.

You will need a piece of paper and a pen, a lighter or matches, and a fireproof bowl for this exercise.

SAFETY FIRST

Always perform this ritual in a safe and well-ventilated area.
Never leave the fire unattended.
Have a fire extinguisher or a bucket of water nearby, just in case.

1| Find somewhere you can sit comfortably and undisturbed. When you're ready to begin, take a few deep breaths.

2| Start to write down any limiting beliefs, fears, or anxieties that are getting in the way of your dreams. Don't hold back; let it all out.

3| Next, take a moment to express gratitude for the lessons these beliefs have taught you, even if they weren't always pleasant. Acknowledge that you're ready to let them go and embrace a more positive mindset.

4| Finally, carefully hold the paper over the fireproof bowl, and set the paper alight before quickly setting it down in the bowl to burn. As it burns, imagine your limiting beliefs dissolving into smoke, freeing you from their grip.

5| Repeat this ritual whenever you feel stuck or weighed down by negativity in order to reset your mindset and move forward with renewed energy.

Tips for Letting Go

Letting go of what no longer serves you can be challenging, but it's essential for personal growth and creating space for new possibilities. Letting go can take time, so try these tips to help you develop your practice:

BE PATIENT WITH YOURSELF

It can be challenging to let big things go. Actively revisit this exercise whenever you're feeling discouraged.

KEEP PRACTICING

The more you practice letting go, the easier it'll become.

GUIDED MEDITATIONS ARE YOUR FRIEND

If you are struggling and need a little help, try a guided meditation specifically for letting go. There are many free ones online.

JOURNAL PROMPTS TO BREAK FREE FROM SELF-DOUBT

1
What does the most confident, badass version of myself do differently to what I do now?

2
How can I start to act like this version of myself, even in small ways?

3
What tiny action I can take right now that proves to myself that I'm capable and worthy?

4
What are my past successes, big or small?

5
What would I do if I knew I couldn't fail?

6
What small step can I take today to move forward despite my doubts?

DAILY AFFIRMATIONS TO BREAK FREE FROM SELF-DOUBT

I am resilient and learn from my mistakes.

Failure is simply a stepping-stone to success.

I am unique and have my own path to follow.

I celebrate my own achievements and those of others.

I deserve love, happiness, and success.

I am valuable and have much to offer the world.

I believe in my ability to overcome any obstacle.

Discover Your Power

Shedding layers of self-doubt is like peeling back an onion, revealing the amazing, authentic you underneath. It takes courage and self-love to dismantle those old beliefs that have been holding you back.

As you identify and challenge those negative thoughts, you're creating space for a whole new, empowered version of yourself to step into the spotlight.

Your story is still being written, and you have the power to shape it with every choice you make. By focusing on personal growth and believing in yourself, you can rewrite your narrative and unleash your full potential.

This process isn't about being perfect; it's about giving yourself permission to be human. It's okay to have moments of doubt along the way. The key is to recognize those feelings, give yourself a break, and then keep moving forward with strength and determination toward your goals.

You've already taken a huge step by beginning to understand and overcome your self-doubt. Just as shedding layers of self-doubt reveals your authentic self, so too does overcoming internal barriers open doors to new possibilities. Imagine these limitations as closed doors, blocking your path to a life of joy and fulfillment. By addressing your fears and developing self-belief, you can begin to unlock these doors, revealing a world of opportunities waiting to be explored. Now, it's time to truly own your power and embrace the magic that's been inside you all along.

In the next chapter, you'll discover how to harness your incredible inner strength and learn how to begin channeling that energy into creating the life you desire, opening the door to your dreams. Let go of the past, embrace the present moment, and step confidently through the doors that lead to your dreams.

Find
YOUR
Inner
POWER

In this chapter, we'll dive into the heart of manifestation: understanding the power of your thoughts and working with the Law of Attraction. You'll learn how to align your inner world with the outer world to create a life of abundance, and by understanding the connection between your thoughts, feelings, and the reality you experience, you'll gain the tools to become the master architect of your own destiny.

Finding Your Inner Power

So far, you've dug deep to uncover your true desires and face any pesky doubts that may be standing in your way. Now, get ready to tap into the real magic of manifestation: the power that lies within you.

We all have an incredible wellspring of potential within us, and manifestation is all about harnessing the immense power of your thoughts, beliefs, and intentions.

When you ignite this inner magic, you become an active creator of your reality. And it's not just about you; the universe has its own magic too. Think of it like a giant cosmic echo chamber, where the energy of the universe is constantly at play, and your thoughts and feelings are just like magnets drawing in experiences and situations that match your vibe.

Now, it's time to blend your inner power with the energy of the universe. In this step, you'll discover the two core "laws" of manifestation—the Law of Attraction and the Law of Assumption—and exercises that use them to help you bridge the gap between your dreams and reality. Once you begin to understand how these laws work, you'll see that manifestation is

less about waiting for things to happen and more about becoming a participant in your life's unfolding.

When you use the Law of Attraction, you draw to you what resonates with your energy. The Law of Assumption, on the other hand, teaches you to act as if your desires have already manifested. Together, these laws work in harmony, guiding you toward what you seek. The key is consistency and aligning your thoughts, actions, and energy every day, creating a magnetic field of possibility around you.

THE LAW OF ATTRACTION

Deep within you lies an incredible power: the ability to transform your world using your mind. This is manifestation, and it starts with understanding that everything in the universe, including you, is made up of energy vibrating at a certain frequency.

Building off of this understanding (which is also known as the Law of Vibration), the Law of Attraction is a fundamental manifestation technique and is the principle that the energy you put out into the world comes back to you. Whether you're consciously aware of it or not, this law is always at play, shaping your experiences and bringing you situations that match your dominant thoughts and feelings.

While the Law of Attraction has gained major attention in the twenty-first century, ancient wisdom traditions and philosophers have been talking about the concept of "like attracts like" for centuries. The New Thought movement in the early 1900s brought the idea that our thoughts can influence reality into the mainstream. Then, in 2006, the book *The Secret* introduced millions of people to the Law of Attraction. Today, it's still inspiring and empowering people all over the world to create lives filled with abundance and joy.

Imagine the universe as a mirror reflecting back to you the energy you put out into the world. When you focus on positive thoughts, feelings of abundance, and belief in your desires, you vibrate at a high frequency, which acts like a beacon, attracting experiences and situations that match that positive energy.

On the other hand, if you dwell on negativity, fear, or doubt, you

vibrate at a lower frequency. This lower vibration then attracts experiences that match that negativity, making it seem like things are going against you.

While we can't always control what happens to us and "negative" thoughts and emotions are a part of being human, by consciously choosing your thoughts and emotions, you can unlock the doors to the positive experiences you desire and create the reality you dream of.

The beauty of this principle is that it places the power of creation firmly in your hands. You aren't a passive observer, but an active participant in shaping your reality.

THE LAW OF ASSUMPTION

Another core manifestation technique is the Law of Assumption. A cornerstone of manifestation practices, the Law of Assumption was initially brought to light by Neville Goddard, a mid-twentieth century author and lecturer who captivated audiences with his ideas about the power of the human imagination.

Based off the theory that whatever you assume to be true will ultimately become your reality, this is the principle that you have the power to manifest anything you desire simply by thinking and feeling as if you already possess it.

The Law of Assumption doesn't just stop at believing your desires are possible; it asks you to live as if they're already your reality. It's about more than just saying, "I will get that promotion"; it's about feeling the excitement and gratitude of already having it.

This technique might sound out there at first, but the idea of it is to create such a strong feeling of already having what you desire that it becomes your dominant vibration. You're essentially tricking your subconscious mind into believing it's already true, which then aligns your energy with that reality and draws it closer to you, like a magnet.

Essentially, the Law of Assumption is about feeling the emotions, embodying the mindset, and taking the actions of the person you want to become. It's like acting out a role until it becomes second nature. You step into the character of your future self, the one who already has everything they desire, and you start living from that place of fulfillment and gratitude.

The next section is all about experiencing your dreams as reality. In the following exercises, you'll learn how to use visualization to create mental movies that are so real, your subconscious mind will start to believe them. You'll explore ways to develop a deep sense of gratitude for everything you already have, which opens the door for even more amazing things to come your way. Through these exercises, you'll start to embody the feelings and mindset of someone who's already living their best life.

FINDING YOUR INNER POWER

ALIGN WITH YOUR AUTHENTIC SELF VISUALIZATION

To begin working with the Law of Attraction to manifest your desires, you first need to align with the most authentic version of yourself, as this will help you find your true inner power.

Continuing on from your work breaking free from self-doubt, this means shedding the layers of conditioning and expectations that may cloud your true essence and embracing the unique individual that resides within.

This visualization exercise will help you get started.

1| Settle into a quiet space where you can relax completely. Close your eyes, take a few deep breaths, and let your body and mind unwind.

2| Imagine yourself wearing a mask. What does it look like? What is it hiding? Perhaps it's the mask of perfection, or the one that hides your vulnerability. See yourself wearing different masks for different situations, each one concealing your true essence.

3| Now, gently remove those masks, one by one. Imagine those masks dissolving into the air, freeing you from the roles you no longer need to play.

4| With the masks gone, connect with the source of your strength within, and notice the qualities that make you unique and powerful.

5| Declare to the universe, "This is me."

Tips for Connecting with Your True Self

Self-reflection is like taking a journey inward and is a chance to really get to know yourself on a deeper level. It's about paying attention to your thoughts, feelings, and experiences, and noticing any patterns that reveal your true self. Here are a couple of ways to start that journey:

JOURNAL

Set aside some time each day to write freely about whatever's on your mind. Don't worry about grammar or making sense, just let your thoughts flow onto the page. Look back over your entries later and see whether there are any recurring themes or patterns that give you insights into your true self.

PRACTICE MINDFULNESS AND MEDITATION

Find a quiet space where you can sit comfortably and focus on your breath. Let your thoughts come and go without judgment, just observing them like clouds passing by. You can also practice mindfulness during everyday activities like eating, walking, or even washing dishes. It's about being fully present in the moment, noticing what you're sensing, feeling, and thinking.

FIND YOUR TRUE NORTH EXERCISE

To truly embrace your authentic self, it's essential to identify the core values that resonate most deeply with your soul.

Your core values are like your personal guiding stars and are the unshakable principles that light up your path and help you make choices that feel right. They're the compass that points you towards your truest north, ensuring that your actions and decisions align with your authentic self.

In this exercise, you'll find your true north and inner power.

You will need your journal and a pen, and sticky notes for this exercise.

1| Find somewhere you can sit comfortably and undisturbed. When you're ready to begin, take a few deep breaths.

2| Open your journal to a new page and take a few moments to think about your positive qualities and which values really resonate with you. Note them down.

3| If you're struggling, you can use the list of values opposite to help inspire you (but remember, your core values are unique to you).

4| Once you're finished, look over your list and notice which values really light you up, which ones feel like a deep truth within you.

5| Choose the ones that feel most aligned with your authentic self, and write them down on sticky notes, placing them somewhere you can see them daily.

AUTHENTICITY
ADVENTURE Balance
Compassion
COURAGE Creativity
Curiosity FREEDOM
Kindness Growth
HUMOR HONESTY
LOYALTY Love
Passion OPENNESS
RESILIENCE Respect
Spirituality TRUST

Guided Meditation to Meet Your Future Self

Now that you've established your values and connected a bit more with your authentic self, it's time to imagine how these values look in your future self, who has become the most empowered, successful version of yourself. This meditation will take you on a journey to meet them, ready to use the Law of Assumption to step into their reality and make it yours.

1| Find a comfortable position sitting or lying down.

2| Gently close your eyes and take a few deep breaths. Inhale slowly and deeply, filling your lungs with life-giving energy. Exhale, releasing any tension or worry.

3| Continue to breathe and imagine yourself surrounded by a warm, golden light. Feel it soothing your body, calming your mind, and opening your heart.

4| Picture yourself standing at the edge of a beautiful forest path. As you step onto the path, notice the lush greenery, the sunlight filtering through the leaves, and the sweet scent of wildflowers in the air.

5| Follow the path deeper into the forest, feeling a sense of excitement and anticipation building within you. As you walk,

notice how the path begins to transform, becoming wider, smoother, and easier to navigate.

6| Ahead, you see a clearing bathed in sunlight. In the center of the clearing stands a figure: your future self. This is the you who has achieved your dreams, overcome your challenges, and blossomed into your fullest potential.

7| Take a moment to observe your future self. Notice their posture, their expression, and the energy they radiate. What do they look like? How do they carry themselves? What emotions do you feel in their presence?

8| Approach your future self and greet them with a warm smile. Feel the love and acceptance they have for you, and ask them any questions you have about your journey or your goals. Listen carefully to the wise and loving guidance they have to offer you.

9| Take a few moments to simply be with your future self, absorbing their wisdom and energy. Feel the weight of their accomplishments, the confidence in their stride, and the wisdom in their eyes.

10| When you are ready, thank them for their guidance and support, and slowly begin to walk back along the path, carrying the wisdom and inspiration you have received.

11| As you emerge from the forest, carry the feeling of empowerment and possibility with you.

12| Take a few deep breaths, grounding yourself in the present moment, and when you are ready, open your eyes and carry the magic of this meditation with you throughout your day.

MIRROR, MIRROR SELF-LOVE RITUAL

Mirror work is a powerful manifestation tool, as it is a way to face your own reflection and speak your dreams into existence. It might feel a bit awkward at first, but with practice, this exercise can boost your self-confidence and supercharge your manifestation game.

This exercise is also a simple yet transformative way to step into the shoes of your future self. Your mirror becomes more than just a tool for checking your appearance, and becomes a space for speaking your dreams and desires into existence through positive affrmations, reprogramming your subconscious mind.

You will need a mirror for this exercise.

1| You're going to be repeating positive affirmations to yourself in the mirror, so take some time to choose some affirmations that really speak to your desires. These should be statements that reflect the reality you want to create, like "I am worthy of love and abundance." You may like to use any affirmations you created on page 50.

2| When you're ready to begin, stand or sit in front of a mirror where you can see your eyes clearly.

3| Take a few deep breaths, look into your eyes, and say your affirmations out loud. Speak with conviction, like you're already living the life of your future self.

4| As you speak, notice any sensations or emotions that come up. Let yourself fully feel the power of your words. Embrace the confidence, joy, and self-love that bubble up.

5| Repeat your affirmations for a few minutes, letting yourself sink deeper into that feeling of already having what you desire.

Tips for Connecting with Your Future Self

As you step into the role of your future self, you're not just play-acting, you're aligning with the very essence of the Law of Assumption. By embodying the qualities and actions of your desired self, you find your inner power and become a magnet for the experiences and opportunities that match your vibration. Here are some additional ways to make this mirror exercise even more powerful:

DRESS THE PART

If your future self has a particular style, try incorporating elements of that style into your wardrobe.

SPEAK THE LANGUAGE

Pay attention to how your future self communicates. Are they eloquent and articulate? Practice speaking in a way that aligns with their communication style.

EMBRACE THE FEELINGS

Allow yourself to feel the emotions associated with being your future self. These emotions will create a powerful energetic attraction towards your desired reality.

SHOWER RITUAL TO MANIFEST YOUR DREAMS

A simple ritual you can do each day to continue practicing the Law of Assumption is this shower visualization. In addition to encouraging you to keep stepping into the role of your future self and tune in to your deepest desires, you'll wash away any stress and negativity from the day.

By making time for this visualization every time you shower, you can tap into the power of your subconscious mind, align your energy with your desires, and manifest your dreams with ease and grace.

1| Step into the shower and let the warm water wash over you.

2| Imagine any tension or worries melting away as you wash your body. Take deep breaths, inhaling the steam and exhaling anything that's weighing you down.

3| Picture your desires in vivid detail. See yourself living the life you dream of, achieving your goals, and experiencing pure joy and fulfillment. Imagine yourself in specific scenarios, using all your senses. What do you see, hear, smell, taste, and feel?

4| As you visualize, let yourself fully experience the emotions that come with achieving your dreams. Let those emotions wash over you like the warm water, filling you with energy and inspiration.

5| When you're ready to finish, take a moment to express gratitude for all the good things already in your life, and thank the universe for its support and guidance. This gratitude creates a positive vibe that attracts even more blessings into your life.

Tips for Embodying Your Future Self Daily

The warm water and the rhythmic sound of the shower in this ritual can help you relax, making you more open to visualization and positive affirmations. Engaging all your senses also creates a richer, more powerful experience, making it easier for your subconscious mind to accept your desired reality as true. Here are some further ways you can connect with your future self daily:

AFFIRMATION POWER

Repeat positive affirmations each day to strengthen your beliefs and program your subconscious mind for success.

VISUALIZE AND FEEL

Take a few minutes each day to vividly imagine yourself living your dream life. Don't just see it, feel it. What emotions are you experiencing? Joy? Gratitude? Freedom? The more you connect with those feelings, the more you'll attract those experiences into your reality.

WALK THE WALK

Dress like your future self to help you step into their shoes.

JOURNAL PROMPTS TO FIND YOUR INNER POWER

1
Who do I admire for their manifesting abilities?

2
What qualities do they embody that I'd like to cultivate in myself?

3
What are my biggest fears, and how can I overcome them to step into my power?

4
How can I use my power to make the world a better place?

5
What makes me feel truly powerful?

6
What does my inner voice tell me about my power?

7
What does my most powerful self look and act like?

DAILY AFFIRMATIONS TO FIND YOUR INNER POWER

I am a powerful creator.

My inner magic is limitless.

I trust my intuition and follow my inner guidance.

I believe in my magic and my ability to create my reality.

I am confident in my choices and trust my path.

I effortlessly attract my desires into my life.

I am a magnet for miracles and abundance.

I transform challenges into opportunities for growth.

My inner magic guides me through any obstacle.

Believe It, Receive It

One of the biggest steps toward finding your inner magic is realizing just how powerful your subconscious mind is when it comes to manifesting your dreams. It's not just about surface-level wishes or fleeting desires; true manifestation comes from deep within, from the core beliefs you hold about yourself and the world.

Your subconscious is like the canvas where your dreams come to life. By developing a positive mindset using the Law of Attraction and the Law of Assumption, and aligning your thoughts and actions with your values and goals, you start rewriting the story your subconscious tells you. When you wholeheartedly believe in your dreams and feel the joy and gratitude as if they've already happened, you're sending a powerful signal to the universe, and you radiate an irresistible energy that matches your deepest desires and draws them closer.

In the next step, you'll be taking inspired action to help pull these energies and opportunities toward you. To fully harness this power, you'll explore how to take steps that align with your inner vision, and further propel you toward your dreams with purpose and intention, and make your manifestations a reality.

The power of your subconscious mind is undeniable. It acts like a powerful filter, shaping your reality based on your deepest held beliefs. When you consistently focus on your goals and believe in the possibility of achieving your dreams, you begin to reprogram your subconscious mind, attracting opportunities and experiences that align with your desires.

By developing a positive and unwavering belief in yourself and the universe, you create a powerful vibration that attracts the abundance you seek.

Take
INSPIRED
Action

Make YOUR VISION a Reality

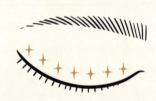

Imagine yourself riding the waves of life. You paddle with intention, choose the right wave to catch, and work with the power of the ocean, allowing it to carry you toward your destination. In this chapter, we'll delve into the art of inspired action. Get ready to ride the waves of opportunity with confidence and grace, trusting that the universe will help guide you with the wind on your side.

Taking Inspired Action

You've laid the groundwork for your manifestations by clarifying your desires, developing a positive mindset, and finding your inner power. Now, it's time to take the next exhilarating step on your manifestation journey: taking inspired action.

But what exactly is inspired action, and how do we distinguish it from ordinary, everyday actions? Inspired action is like that tingly feeling you get when you know something amazing is about to happen. It's when your heart skips a beat and you can't wait to take the next step. It's that inner knowing that you're on the right track. But how do you know when you're feeling inspired action? That's where your intuition comes in.

Intuition is like your very own magic compass guiding you toward your dreams. It's that inner voice that guides you toward the right choices for you and helps open doors to incredible opportunities.

Every time you feel that nudge from within, you're discovering a new path, unlocking a hidden part of yourself, and moving closer to the treasure you seek.

Trusting your intuition is like having a superpower.

Sometimes, it might urge you to do something that seems totally random, but trust that it's all part of a bigger plan you can't quite see yet. At other times, it might just be a feeling of peace or excitement about a certain path. Pay close attention to those subtle hints and gut feelings that push you in the right direction.

When you listen to that inner voice, you're stepping onto the path of inspired action, and that's where the magic really starts to happen.

This chapter will help you tap into your intuition and take inspired action that builds upon all of the good work that you've done so far in this book. Get ready to take concrete steps that will move you forward!

TAKING INSPIRED ACTION

CREATE YOUR MANIFESTATION ROAD MAP

Ready to turn your dreams into reality? Let's create a manifestation road map. Think of it as your GPS for success, guiding you step by step toward your goals.

In this exercise, you'll break down those big dreams into smaller, totally doable steps so they feel less like far-off fantasies and more like an exciting adventure you're about to embark on. This is your personal map to success, so make it totally unique and tailored to your goals. The more detailed and specific you can be, the more powerful this exercise will be.

You will need your journal and a pen for this exercise.

1| Find somewhere you can sit comfortably and undisturbed to create your road map.

2| When you're ready to begin, take a few deep breaths and open your journal to a new page.

3| To begin your road map, write the word "Destination" at the top of your page. Under this heading, write about your ultimate goals or manifestations. Get crystal clear and feel free to refer back to your wish list from step 1 to help. You may find that some of your wishes have changed now that you've completed steps 2 and 3, and that's totally fine.

4| Underneath the destination section, write the words "Where I'm At." Then, write an honest assessment of where you are right now in relation to your goal.

5| Next, write "Milestone Markers" and begin to work out how you can break down your big goals into smaller, achievable milestones. Assign a realistic time frame to each milestone. Don't worry about how you're going to get there yet; just imagine what these milestones are. These milestones will serve as checkpoints along the way that'll keep you motivated, and help create a clear path toward your destination.

6| When you're ready to move on to the next step, write "Action Time" underneath your milestone markers. For each milestone, brainstorm three to five specific actions you can take to reach it. These are the concrete steps you'll take, so take your time with this step and don't be afraid to cross things out and rewrite them. You can create this section over as many days as you need to and can practice the daily shower ritual from page 78 to help you overcome any overwhelm while you do this step.

7| Once you have established your milestone actions, write down "Curveballs and Roadblocks." Then, journal about any potential challenges or obstacles that might pop up. Jot these down on your map, along with possible solutions or detours you could take if needed.

8| Finally, write the heading "Check In and Level Up." This is an area where you can regularly review your manifestation road map, adding new steps, adjusting milestones, and celebrating your wins along the way. This section should be a living document that will grow and change with you.

Feeling Stuck?

If you're struggling to create your manifestation map, the following example road maps may help inspire you.

MANIFESTATION ROAD MAP FOR A DREAM JOB

DESTINATION

✦ Secure a fulfilling and well-paying job as a graphic designer at a top creative agency within the next two years

WHERE I'M AT

✦ Currently working as a freelance designer, building a portfolio, and networking within the industry

MILESTONE MARKERS

✦ Have a beautiful, up-to-date portfolio created within the next month
✦ Have attended two industry networking events over the next three months
✦ Have applied to five dream companies over the next year

ACTION TIME

- Update my portfolio with my latest and best work
- Utilize my freelance connections by reaching out to my best past clients to inquire about job vacancies
- Research and apply to my dream companies
- Submit proposals on job boards and network on LinkedIn
- Reach out to a recruiter within my field
- Prepare an elevator pitch for myself and follow up with new contacts
- Tailor my résumé and cover letter, and practice interviews
- Attend networking events such as research events

CURVEBALLS AND ROADBLOCKS

- Rejection from dream companies
  Solution: Seek feedback, continue improving skills and portfolio, and apply to more companies
- Freelance projects take up too much time
  Solution: Prioritize dream job applications and set boundaries with freelance clients

CHECK IN AND LEVEL UP

- Review progress weekly, celebrate small wins (for example, positive feedback on portfolio), and adjust actions as needed

MANIFESTATION ROAD MAP FOR A HEALTHY LIFESTYLE

DESTINATION

✦ Achieve and maintain a healthy, energized-feeling body and improve overall well-being

WHERE I'M AT

✦ Currently struggling with unhealthy eating habits, feeling sluggish, and lacking motivation to exercise

MILESTONE MARKERS

✦ Eating three healthy meals per day within the next two weeks

✦ Getting 7–8 hours of quality sleep each night within the next month

✦ Exercising three or four times per week within the next two months

✦ Reducing stress levels daily through mindfulness practices within the next three months

ACTION TIME

- Create and consume healthy meals that I enjoy by meal prepping on weekends, finding healthy recipes that I love, and swapping unhealthy snacks for fruits and vegetables
- Encourage myself to exercise by finding enjoyable activities (such as dancing and hiking), joining a gym or fitness class, and finding a workout buddy
- Reduce stress by meditating daily, practicing deep breathing, and spending time in nature
- Get quality sleep by establishing a consistent sleep schedule, creating a relaxing bedtime routine, and avoiding screens before bed

CURVEBALLS AND ROADBLOCKS

- Busy schedule makes it hard to exercise
  Solution: Incorporate short workouts throughout the day, prioritizing exercise in the morning
- Cravings for unhealthy food
  Solution: Keep healthy snacks readily available, find healthy alternative to favorite treats, and allow myself the occasional treat

CHECK IN AND LEVEL UP

- Track progress in a journal weekly and celebrate victories (such as increased energy levels), adjusting plan as needed

INTUITION CHECK-IN

Now that you've drafted your manifestation road map and are ready to begin taking inspired action toward achieving your goals, it's a good time to check in with your intuition to make sure your action plan is aligned with your soul's purpose and the universe. By checking in with your gut and prioritizing actions that feel aligned and exciting before you fully dive into action, you'll supercharge your manifestation journey.

This exercise will help you tap into your gut feeling to check that the steps you have planned will light you up and get you closer to your goals.

You will need your journal and a pen for this exercise.

1| Find somewhere you can sit comfortably and undisturbed.

2| When you're ready to begin, take a few deep breaths.

3| Open up your journal to your manifestation road map and draw your attention to the actions section.

4| On a new page, rewrite down three to five of these actions in a list. You may like to select actions that align with the first milestone markers you want to meet.

5| Now, go through each action and rate it on a scale of 1–10 for each of these categories:

✦ Excitement/Motivation: How excited and motivated do you feel about taking this action? (1 being not at all excited, 10 being extremely excited)

✦ Ease/Flow: Does this action feel easy and natural, or forced and difficult? (1 being very difficult, 10 being effortless)

✦ **Alignment with Values:** Does this action align with your core values and who you truly are? (1 being not aligned at all, 10 being perfectly aligned)

6| Once you're finished scoring your actions, reflect on the results and look at the ratings for each one. Actions with high scores in all three categories are likely inspired actions that aligned with your intuition and purpose. These are the actions you want to prioritize, so underline them.

7| Next, see whether you have any results with mixed scores. Actions with mixed scores may require further reflection, so if you have any, ask yourself and write about:

✦ Is there any resistance or fear holding me back from this action?

✦ Can I modify this action to make it feel more aligned and exciting?

✦ Is there a different action that might be a better fit for me right now?

8| Finally, assess whether you have any actions with low scores, as these may not be the most inspired choices at this time. If so, it's okay to let go of these actions for now and focus on the ones that truly resonate with you, or, if they're something you feel you must do, see the next two exercises for guidance.

THE INSPIRED ACTION DARE

It can be scary to take the first steps on your manifestation road map, especially if some of them are difficult, so this exercise is all about shaking things up and taking a bold leap toward your dreams. It's time to face your fears, embrace the unknown, and unleash your inner daredevil.

You will need your journal and a pen for this exercise.

1| Find somewhere you can sit comfortably and undisturbed. When you're ready to begin, take a few deep breaths.

2| Open your journal to your answers for the intuition check-in exercise on page 96 and select any low or medium scoring actions. If you didn't do so during the previous exercise, identify and write down any fears or resistance around the action.

3| Now, reframe that fear as a challenge, a dare to yourself. Instead of thinking, "I'm afraid to do this," think, "I dare myself to do this!" This simple shift in perspective can empower you to take action.

4| Give yourself a deadline to complete the dare and write it down alongside your dare, as this creates a sense of urgency and accountability. Choose a time frame that feels challenging yet achievable.

5| When the moment comes to take the leap, take a deep breath, trust your gut, and take action.

Tips for Taking the Plunge

You did it! You faced your fears, stepped outside your comfort zone, and took a bold leap toward your dreams. Now, let's reflect on what you learned from this experience and how it can fuel your journey even further.

ANALYZE THE OUTCOME

Did your dare unfold as expected? Were there any surprises or unexpected challenges? What did you learn about yourself and your ability to handle discomfort?

KEEP MOVING FORWARD

Use this experience as fuel to propel you forward. What's the next step you're ready to take? How can you continue to push your boundaries and expand your comfort zone?

CELEBRATE YOUR COURAGE

After completing your dare, take a moment to acknowledge and celebrate your courage. You stepped outside your comfort zone and took a bold step toward your dreams! Reflect on what you learned from the experience and how it has empowered you.

THE INSPIRED ACTION REWARD SYSTEM

Now that you're beginning to put your actions into practice, do you want to stay motivated and make taking action even more fun?

This exercise is all about creating a reward system that celebrates your progress and keeps you inspired. It's time to treat yourself like the manifesting superstar you are.

You will need your journal and a pen for this exercise.

1| Find somewhere you can sit comfortably and undisturbed. When you're ready to begin, take a few deep breaths.

2| Open your journal to a new page and write down any actions you are currently working on or are yet to take.

3| Write down a reward you are going to give yourself for completing each action. If you're struggling to think of a reward, ask yourself: What makes me feel happy, celebrated, and motivated? Choose rewards that excite you and align with your values. These could be small indulgences like a special coffee, a relaxing bath, or a new book, or bigger experiences like a weekend getaway, a concert, or a spa day.

Tips for Celebrating Your Wins

You've set your goals, begun to crush those milestones, and now it's time to celebrate. Don't forget, acknowledging your achievements is a key part of manifesting. It keeps those good vibes flowing, boosts your confidence, and shows the universe you're ready for even more amazing things. Here are some tips to help you celebrate:

MAKE IT MEANINGFUL

Connect specific actions to specific rewards. For example, "If I complete three networking calls this week, I'll treat myself to a massage." This creates a clear connection between your efforts and your rewards.

ENJOY THE PROCESS

As you take inspired action and achieve your goals, make time to truly savor your rewards. Acknowledge your progress, celebrate your wins, and appreciate the journey.

CREATE A VISUAL TRACKER

You may like to create a visual tracker to monitor your progress and celebrate your wins. This could be a chart, a calendar, or a vision board where you can mark off each completed action.

THE "UNIVERSE, SHOW ME A SIGN" CHALLENGE

Taking inspired action is more than just checking things off your to-do list; it's also about aligning your actions with your soul's purpose and the energies of the universe.

The universe sends us messages in many forms. The remaining exercises in this step will help you actively seek guidance from the universe and build trust in its subtle messages, so that you can use this power to help further motivate and inspire your actions.

You will need your journal and a pen for this exercise.

1| Find somewhere you can sit comfortably and undisturbed. When you're ready to begin, take a few deep breaths.

2| Open your journal to a new page and write down anything on your manifestation journey that you are struggling with.

3| Now, you are going to ask the universe for its help. Write down a question you want guidance on. For example, "Should I pursue this new business opportunity?"

4| Next, write down and request a sign from the universe. For example, "Universe, please show me a yellow butterfly if this opportunity is aligned with my highest good." Be very clear about what sign you're looking for.

5| Try to remain aware of your surroundings as you go about your day-to-day life to see whether the universe gives you your sign.

6| If you spot your sign, take a moment to appreciate it and thank the universe, and use the guidance to take your next step.

Tips for Recognizing Signs from the Universe

The universe might send you various signs of encouragement on your path to manifestation, and these signs can take many forms. But here are some common ones to look out for:

REPETITIVE NUMBERS

Seeing the same number sequence repeatedly, like 11:11 or your birth date, can be a sign from the universe. Look up the meaning of these numbers to see whether they resonate with your current desires.

SERENDIPITOUS ENCOUNTERS

Bumping into an old friend who offers unexpected advice or finding a book that perfectly aligns with your current goals could be a sign.

SYMBOLIC ANIMALS

Pay attention to recurring encounters with animals that hold special meaning. A majestic butterfly might symbolize transformation, while a persistent owl could represent wisdom and discernment.

OUT-OF-THE-BLUE PHRASES

Hearing a song lyric or a snippet of conversation that perfectly reflects your desires could be a sign. Trust that these messages are meant for you.

THE COSMIC SCAVENGER HUNT

Are you struggling with making decisions on your manifestation journey, and feel like the universe isn't sending you any signs? Let's play detective. If you are worried you're not receiving any signs of guidance from the universe, this fun game can help you spot any hidden signs and synchronicities that may be pointing you toward your goals.

Remember: this is a playful game, so don't worry about taking it too seriously. The more you practice looking for signs, the better you'll become at deciphering the cosmic clues that surround you.

You will need your journal and a pen for this exercise.

1| Write down a specific question that you'd like guidance from the universe on, like, "What's the next step toward my dream career?"

2| Write down three to five potential answers to this question, and allocate a sign to each answer. These signs could be anything from specific numbers, animals, or symbols, to more general feelings or vibes.

3| Consciously go out into your day and pay attention to the world around you, from the license plates you see to the conversations you overhear. If you struggle to stay present in your day-to-day life, you may like to go on a short walk specifically for this exercise.

4| Each time you notice something that resonates with your sign list, give the universe a mental high five and take a moment to reflect on its meaning.

Tips for Communicating with the Universe

The universe is always talking to us and dropping little clues and hints along our path. When you actively look for these signs and pay attention to them, you're basically strengthening your intuition—that gut feeling that always seems to know what's up. Here's how to further strengthen the connection:

BE SPECIFIC

The more specific your questions and answers, the clearer the sign will be.

TRUST YOUR INTUITION

If something feels like a sign, even if it's not exactly what you asked for, trust your gut and explore its meaning. Likewise, if you find yourself looking for one sign more than others, or are actively avoiding another, that is a sign.

DON'T FORCE IT

If you don't receive a sign right away, don't get discouraged. The universe works in its own timing.

THE DREAM DECODER

Ever feel like your dreams are trying to tell you something? They totally are! In addition to looking for signs that you're on the right path from the universe in your waking life, you can also look for signs in your subconscious world.

This exercise will help you tap into the messages in your dreams, ready to use them to help achieve your goals.

You will need your journal and a pen for this exercise.

1| Place your journal and a pen by your bedside, ready to journal about your dreams when you wake up.

2| Before you fall asleep, take a few moments to focus on a specific goal or question you'd like guidance from the universe on. Imagine yourself achieving this goal, feeling the positive emotions associated with it. Then, with a clear mind, set your intention to receive dream messages related to it, before drifting off to sleep.

3| Upon waking, immediately jot down any dream fragments, feelings, or symbols you remember. Don't worry about perfect grammar or complete sentences, just capture the essence.

4| Later in the day, revisit your dream notes. What symbols or metaphors stand out? Do any recurring themes or emotions emerge? Consider what these elements might represent in relation to the goal you focused on, and take any actions you feel inspired to take.

Tips for Decoding Your Dreams

You've set your intention, captured those fleeting dream fragments, and now you're ready to decipher their hidden meanings. Here are some tips to help you unlock the wisdom within your dreams:

CHECK OUT COMMON DREAM SYMBOLS

Want to know what that recurring snake or flying dream might mean? Do some research! Books, websites, and apps can give you clues.

FEEL THE FEELS

Pay attention to how you felt in the dream. Your emotions can give you big hints about the dream's message.

TRUST YOUR INNER KNOWING

As you interpret your dreams, pay attention to your gut feelings. What intuitive whispers arise? Don't overthink it; simply allow your inner wisdom to guide your understanding of your dreams' messages.

JOURNAL PROMPTS TO TAKE INSPIRED ACTION

1

What's one small step I can take today to move closer to my dream job or career path?

2

How can I show up more authentically and express my needs in my relationships?

3

What's one healthy habit I can incorporate into my routine today to support my overall well-being?

4

What creative project have I been putting off? What's one small action I can take today to get started?

5

Are there any signs I've noticed that seem particularly relevant to my goals?

6

What actions can I take in response to these signs?

DAILY AFFIRMATIONS TO TAKE INSPIRED ACTION

I am taking inspired action toward my dreams every day.

My actions are aligned with my intentions and desires.

I release procrastination and embrace momentum.

I trust my intuition to guide me toward the right opportunities.

I am open to receiving inspiration and taking aligned action.

I am filled with energy and enthusiasm for pursuing my dreams.

I celebrate my progress and acknowledge my achievements.

I step outside my comfort zone with confidence and curiosity.

I focus on one action at a time and celebrate my progress.

I am passionate about creating the life I desire.

Making Your Dreams Happen

This step was all about turning your dreams into reality by taking inspired action. You've learned to break down those big, audacious dreams into manageable steps, climbing that mountain with focus and determination. You've tapped into your intuition, that inner guide leading you toward exciting new possibilities. And you've unleashed the power of momentum, building unstoppable force with consistent action.

This journey is about embracing the process and trusting in your own power. Now, with a solid foundation of inspired action, it's time to surrender to the magic of the universe.

In the next and final step, we'll dive deep into the art of surrendering, letting go of control, and allowing the universe to work its wonders.

You'll learn to release doubt and worry, embrace a deep sense of trust that everything is unfolding perfectly (even when it might not seem like it), and practice gratitude and thanks for everything you've manifested already in order to attract even more abundance.

This last step involves embracing the Law of Detachment. Just as a flower doesn't strive to bloom, but simply allows itself to unfold naturally, so too must we. Detachment isn't about apathy; it's about releasing our attachment to the outcome.

We plant the seeds of our dreams through inspired action, nurture them with consistent effort, and then trust that the universe will orchestrate the perfect unfolding. This doesn't mean we stop taking action, but it means we trust that the universe will support our journey in ways we may not always understand. By surrendering to the divine flow, we open ourselves to unexpected blessings and allow our dreams to blossom with effortless grace.

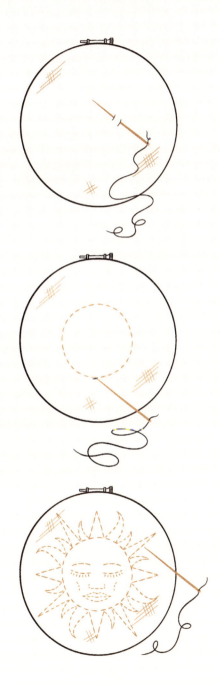

TRUST THE *Universe*

Trust
THE

Process

You've unveiled your wishes, broken free from self-doubt, ignited your inner magic, and started taking inspired action. Now, it's time to surrender to the unfolding of your dreams. This final step is all about trusting the universe. In it, we'll explore how to surrender to divine timing, release the need for control, and develop faith and thanks for the universe. Let's delve into how wisdom, trust, and gratitude can accelerate your manifestation journey.

Trusting the Universe

Trust can be a tricky concept. How do you truly believe in something unseen that hasn't materialized yet? The answer lies in understanding the power of your own energy.

When you develop unwavering trust, you align your own energy with the abundant flow of the universe. This positive shift fosters trust in the universe's ability to provide for your desires.

As you learned in step 3 with the Law of Attraction, the universe responds to the frequency you broadcast: your thoughts, emotions, and beliefs. You've also proven by now through your hard work that manifestation doesn't mean sitting back and waiting for your dreams to magically fall into your lap; it's about taking inspired action.

This final step in your manifestation journey is about a subtle shift in mindset, moving you from any forceful "I need to control everything" thinking to a more graceful "I trust the process" mode.

When you develop unwavering trust, you align your own energy with the abundant flow of the universe. It might feel a bit uncomfortable at first switching to this mindset, as we're so used

to thinking that control equals success, and many of us crave predictability and a straight path to our goals. But the universe works in mysterious ways, with a cosmic rhythm far grander than any plan we could come up with.

Think of your manifestation journey like sculpting a masterpiece. You start with a clear vision, carefully shaping the rough outline with your goals and inspired actions. But as the piece takes form, you also listen to your intuition, letting the natural beauty of the material guide your hand.

Trusting the magic of manifestation is similar, and in this final step on your journey, you'll learn how to use the Law of Detachment and practice gratitude to create a deep well of trust in yourself and the universe, which in turn will help attract even more abundance toward you.

THE LAW OF DETACHMENT

The Law of Detachment is an essential key to unlocking the full flow of abundance.

This manifestation principle states that by releasing your attachment to specific outcomes, you open yourself to receive your desires in the most perfect and abundant way possible. While it encourages you to set clear intentions and take inspired action, it also asks you to let go of the need to control every detail. This surrender allows the universe to work its magic, often bringing forth manifestations that surpass your wildest dreams.

Imagine you're planting a beautiful garden. You carefully select the seeds, prepare the soil, and water them with love. But you don't obsess over every tiny sprout, demanding that they grow in a specific way or at a specific pace. You trust the natural process of growth, knowing that with the right conditions, the seeds will blossom into their full potential.

The Law of Detachment operates in a similar way. You set your intentions, take inspired action, and then surrender the outcome to the universe. You trust that the universe with its infinite wisdom and abundance will organize the details in a way that far exceeds your limited human perspective.

This surrender doesn't mean giving up or becoming passive. It's about releasing the need to micromanage and control every aspect of the manifestation process, and about recognizing that the universe has a plan far grander than your own. The first exercises in this step, which are based upon this law, will help you fine-tune your energetic dial to let the

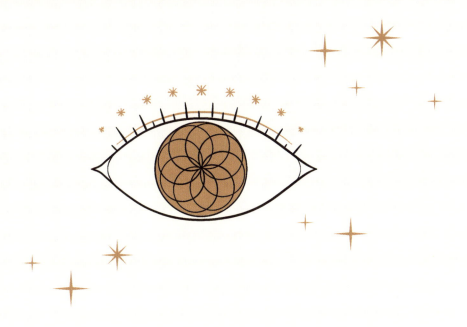

universe guide you even closer to your desires.

The Law of Detachment is about finding inner peace. When we release our grip on the "how" and trust in the universe, a sense of calm settles within us. We're no longer consumed by anxiety or doubt, and this inner peace allows for a more receptive state of being, making us more open to receiving the abundance that flows toward us.

Imagine a serene lake reflecting the beauty of the sky. When the water is still, it mirrors the heavens perfectly. Similarly, when we release our inner turmoil, we become a clear channel for the flow of abundance, allowing our desires to manifest effortlessly.

THE FERTILE GROUND OF GRATITUDE

Practicing gratitude on your manifestation journey is another key component to encouraging more abundance in your life. Gratitude is more than just a polite "thank you"; it's a potent energy that can completely shift your whole outlook on life.

When you actively focus on the good stuff and on all the things you're grateful for, you're essentially switching your vibe from "I don't have enough" to "I have so much to be thankful for!" This opens the floodgates for even more blessings to flow your way, as when you're vibrating at a high frequency of gratitude, you're essentially sending a signal to the universe that you're ready to receive more.

Gratitude is a powerful manifesting tool. It's like saying, "Thank you for all the amazing things in my life, and I'm open to receiving even more!" The more you practice gratitude, the more you'll notice the abundance that surrounds you. It's like training your mind to focus on the positive, creating a powerful magnet for even more blessings to come your way.

You'll start to see opportunities where you once saw obstacles, and you'll attract experiences that align with your newfound sense of appreciation.

Remember: the Law of Attraction states that "like attracts like." By focusing on appreciation and gratitude, you cultivate a positive energy vibration that resonates with the universe's abundance. This positive energy attracts more positive experiences and helps manifest your desires.

Alongside key techniques for practicing the Law of Detachment

in this chapter, you'll find a collection of gratitude practices in this step to help you make gratitude a daily habit, as you watch your life blossom.

You may like to dedicate a special notebook or a digital document to jotting down a few things you're grateful for each day. This could be something as simple as expressing thanks for a warm cup of tea, a supportive friend, or a beautiful sunset. The act of writing down your blessings can help to solidify such simple pleasures in your mind and heart.

RELEASE AND FLOW WATER RITUAL

Ever feel like you're clinging to things that are weighing you down? It's time to let go and embrace the flow.

This ritual uses the power of water to help you release what no longer serves you and open yourself to new possibilities.

You will need a natural body of water and something that floats (like a flower or leaf) for this exercise.

1| Head to your chosen body of water and get comfy.

2| Take a few deep breaths, and connect with the energy of the water.

3| Hold your floating object and imagine all your worries, doubts, or anything you're ready to release flowing into it. Visualize those burdens leaving your mind and body and entering the object.

4| When you're ready, let it go. Gently place the object on the water and watch it float away. As it goes with the flow, imagine your worries drifting away with it, surrendering them to the universe.

5| As your object floats and moves away, take a moment to observe the water. See how effortlessly it moves around obstacles, adapts to its surroundings, and always finds its way? Let that inspire you to trust the universe's guidance.

6| Say a quick thank you to the water and the universe for helping you release those burdens and guiding you toward your dreams.

Tips for Building Trust

As we explored in step 2, doubt and fear are like weeds in the garden of your mind that can prevent your desires from blooming and stop you from trusting. To fully embrace the magic of manifestation, it's essential to uproot these weeds at every stage of your manifestation journey to create a clear and fertile space for your dreams to grow. Here are some ways to help do this:

REMEMBER YOUR WINS

Build trust in yourself by remembering your past successes. Think back to times you overcame challenges, reached your goals, and showed how strong you are. Notice how you learned and grew from setbacks. These past wins prove you can handle challenges and achieve your dreams.

CHALLENGE YOUR THOUGHTS

Are your fears based on reality, or are they simply old stories you're replaying in your mind? Challenge your negative thoughts with evidence to the contrary and reframe them with positive affirmations.

INNER CHILD WORK

Often, our fears and doubts are rooted in childhood experiences. Research ways to connect with your inner child and offer them reassurance and love. This can help heal old wounds and release any longer-term limiting beliefs that might be holding you back.

Release Attachment Meditation

Sometimes on your manifestation journey, you may find you're so pumped about manifesting something amazing that the more you try to force it, the further away it seems. It's like trying to catch a butterfly—the harder you chase it, the more it flits away.

This meditation ritual is all about taking a step back, releasing attachment to outcomes, and trusting in the universe's divine plan to make the magic happen naturally.

You will need a lighter or matches, a candle, and calming music for this exercise.

1| Choose a place where you can relax and won't be disturbed.

2| Light a candle and play some calming music to create a peaceful atmosphere.

3| Close your eyes and take a few deep breaths, focusing on calming your mind and body.

4| Next, visualize your desired outcome in vivid detail, allowing yourself to feel the joy and excitement of its manifestation.

5| Imagine gently releasing your desire into the universe, like a butterfly taking flight or a leaf floating downstream. Feel the weight lifting from your shoulders as you surrender your attachment to the outcome.

6| Trust that the universe has received your message and is orchestrating the perfect path for your desire to manifest.

7| Repeat an affirmation like, "I release this desire with love and trust in the universe's perfect timing."

8| Thank the universe for its unwavering support and open your heart to receiving the unexpected and wondrous ways your desire may unfold.

9| Conclude the ritual by taking a few more deep breaths, basking in the feeling of peace, trust, and surrender.

BURNING BOWL RELEASE RITUAL

In this ritual, you will begin to symbolically burn away attachments to any too-specific outcomes that you are struggling to manifest, allowing space for new possibilities and manifestations. Fire has a raw, magical energy that's both destructive and creative, making it the perfect tool for a manifesting ritual all about letting go.

You will need a fireproof bowl or container, a lighter or matches, and a piece of paper and a pen for this exercise.

> ### SAFETY FIRST
> Always perform this ritual in a safe and well-ventilated area.
> Never leave the fire unattended.
> Have a fire extinguisher or a bucket of water nearby, just in case.

1| Find a safe and well-ventilated space where you can comfortably perform this ritual.

2| On your piece of paper, write down any specific attachments, worries, fears, or limiting beliefs that you wish to release. Be honest and specific, allowing your thoughts to flow freely onto the page.

3| Carefully light the paper and place it in the fireproof bowl, watching as the flames consume your written words. As you do this, visualize your attachments, worries, and fears burning away, dissipating into the universe.

4| As the flames dance, repeat affirmations that resonate with trust and surrender, such as "I release all that no longer serves me" or "I trust in the divine timing of my life."

5| Watch the smoke rising, carrying away the old energies, and feel the lightness and freedom within you as you release what no longer serves you.

Tips for Releasing What No Longer Serves You

This ritual invites you to tap into that fiery power to burn away any negativity that's holding you back. Here are some other ways you can work to let go of what's no longer serving you and step into your manifesting badassery:

PHYSICALLY LET IT GO

If possible, physically remove things from your life that no longer serve you. This could involve decluttering your home.

SAY GOODBYE SYMBOLICALLY

Create a little ritual to let go of the things that aren't helping you anymore. You could write down what you want to release and then tear it up or burn it. You could also imagine yourself letting go of these things like bubbles floating away.

FORGIVE YOURSELF AND OTHERS

Holding on to resentment and anger only harms you. Forgive yourself for past mistakes and forgive others for their transgressions. Forgiveness is not about condoning harmful behavior, but about releasing yourself from the emotional weight of the past.

SHORT DAILY GRATITUDE PRACTICE

Incorporating a daily gratitude practice into your life is not only a great way to start your day with a positive mindset, but also to send a daily message to the universe that you are ready to receive more abundance.

Focusing solely on the end goal can create frustration and impatience. Gratitude allows you to appreciate the journey of manifestation, recognizing the lessons and growth experiences along the way.

To help you actively cultivate an attitude of gratitude, let's explore a simple practice you can incorporate into your daily routine.

You will need a piece of paper and a pen for this exercise.

1| Each morning, find a comfortable seat and take a few deep breaths.

2| When you're ready to begin, take a few moments to reflect on your life.

3| List three things you're grateful for, big or small. It can be anything from your health and loved ones to a delicious cup of coffee or a beautiful sunrise. Savor the feeling of appreciation as you write down each item.

4| Practice this ritual daily. You may find that you have more than three things to write down in no time.

Tips for Practicing Gratitude Daily

By consistently practicing gratitude, you'll cultivate a mindset of abundance and open yourself up to receiving the magic of manifestation in your life. Here are some more ways that you can incorporate daily gratitude into your life:

GRATITUDE FOR YOUR BODY

Take a moment each day to check in with and send love to your body and all it does for you. This can help foster a positive body image and self-love.

GRATITUDE WALKS

Take a walk in nature or your neighborhood and actively look for things to appreciate. Notice the beauty of a flower, the sound of birds singing, or the kindness of a stranger.

GRATITUDE AS A FAMILY PRACTICE

Share gratitude with your family. You could create a gratitude jar that everyone contributes to (see page 130), or simply take turns expressing appreciation for each other at dinner.

GRATITUDE JAR FOR ABUNDANCE

This gratitude jar is a simple way to shift your focus, create a thankful heart, and open the door for even more amazing things to come your way.

Think of this jar as your personal happy vault. Instead of storing cash or jewels in it, you'll fill it with notes about the awesome moments, experiences, and people that make your life special. Every time you add a note, it's like depositing a little bit of joy into your vault, building a physical reminder of all the good stuff in your world.

You will need pieces of paper, a pen, and a glass jar with a lid for this exercise.

1| At the end of the day on a fresh piece of paper, write down three to five things you're grateful for. These can be big or small things, from a delicious meal to a supportive friend.

2| Once you've written down your list, fold it up and seal it in your glass jar.

3| Repeat these steps each day and at the end of the week or month, or when your jar is full, read the notes from your jar. This will reinforce your gratitude and help you see all the abundance that surrounds you.

Tips for Celebrating Abundance

Your gratitude jar isn't just about feeling good in the moment; it's about rewiring your brain to see the positive. When you regularly reflect on the good stuff, you train your mind to look for the silver lining in any situation, even when things get tough. This change in perspective can have a huge impact on your overall happiness, making you more resilient, optimistic, and deeply content.

GET SPECIFIC

Instead of just writing "My family," try writing "The hilarious conversation I had with my sister today" or "The way my dad always knows how to make me laugh." The more detailed you are, the more powerfully you'll connect with those feelings of gratitude.

SHARE YOUR GRATITUDE

Tell someone you appreciate them, leave a kind note for a coworker, or express your thanks to a helpful stranger. Sharing your gratitude amplifies its positive effects and spreads joy to others.

GRATITUDE LETTER TO THE UNIVERSE

Want to deepen your connection with the universe and increase the flow of blessings in your life? This exercise is about expressing your heartfelt gratitude for all the gifts you've received during your manifestation journey as we come to the end of these five steps.

Enjoy this opportunity to reflect on all you've accomplished so far, and write a love letter to the cosmos to acknowledge the intricate dance of experiences that have shaped your journey.

You will need a piece of paper and a pen, or a computer, for this exercise.

1| Seek out a quiet and peaceful environment where you can connect with your inner self and the vastness of the universe.

2| Grab a pen and paper or open up a new document on your computer.

3| Begin writing your letter to the universe, addressing it as a dear friend or a beloved entity. Express your gratitude for all the blessings in your life, both the grand gestures and the subtle nuances.

4| Express your appreciation for the loved ones who are in your life, the mentors who guide you, and even the strangers who have offered kindness and support.

5| Recall the experiences that have shaped you, the adventures that have opened your heart, the challenges that have strengthened you, and the moments of joy that have filled your soul.

6| Acknowledge the opportunities that have come your way, the doors that have opened, and the paths that have unfolded before you.

7| Express gratitude for the abundance that surrounds you, from the beauty of nature to the comforts of your home to the simple pleasures that bring you joy.

8| Once you've finished writing your letter, find a private space where you can read it aloud. As you read, allow yourself to truly feel the emotions of gratitude and appreciation. Let your voice carry your message to the universe.

9| Finally, it's time to symbolically release your letter to the universe, entrusting your gratitude to the cosmic forces. You can choose any of the following methods that resonates with you:

- ✦ Safely burn your letter in a fire pit or fireplace, visualizing your gratitude rising with the smoke and reaching the heavens.
- ✦ Bury your letter in the earth, offering your gratitude to the natural world and entrusting it to the nurturing energy of the soil.
- ✦ Release your letter into a body of water and watch it float away.

JOURNAL PROMPTS TO TRUST THE UNIVERSE

1
What are three things I'm grateful for right now on my manifesting journey?

2
How can I incorporate more gratitude into my life?

3
How can I show more gratitude toward the people around me?

4
When have I previously surrendered to the flow and things turned out amazing?

5
How can I show the universe I trust its plan?

6
What can I do to go with the flow more in my everyday life and manifestation journey?

DAILY AFFIRMATIONS TO TRUST THE UNIVERSE

I am open to receiving the magic of the universe.

The universe is working its magic on my behalf, even when I can't see it.

I trust the timing and unfolding of my desires.

I release any doubts and anxieties, choosing to trust in the process.

Unexpected detours are opportunities for greater manifestation.

I am worthy of receiving all my desires.

I am a powerful co-creator with the universe.

I surrender control and embrace the flow of abundance.

I am filled with gratitude for the blessings already in my life.

Embracing the Magic of the Universe

As you close this chapter—the final of the five manifestation steps—remember that the power to manifest your dreams lies within you.

You've learned to trust the universe, cultivate unwavering belief, and recognize the signs that guide you along the way. You've embraced the art of letting go and discovered the joy of inspired action. Now, it's time to step confidently into the role of co-creator, weaving your intentions with the magic of the universe. Embrace the journey, trust your intuition, and watch your dreams unfold in beautiful and unexpected ways.

As you close this part of the book and step off the pages into your solo manifestation journey, remember this: you are a powerful manifestor, capable of creating a life filled with purpose, joy, and abundance.

The tools and wisdom you've gained within these steps are yours to carry forward, guiding you toward the life you truly desire. Embrace the journey with an open heart, a curious mind, and an unwavering belief in the magic that lies within you.

This is not the end of the journey, but rather the beginning of a lifelong adventure.

Continue to cultivate gratitude and appreciation for the blessings that flow into your life. Celebrate your victories, both big and small, and learn from any perceived setbacks. Remember that the universe is always conspiring in your favor, even when things don't go exactly as planned. Trust in the divine timing of the universe and embrace the unexpected detours that may lead you to even greater opportunities.

Now go forth and manifest a life that is truly extraordinary. You are a powerful creator, and the universe is eager to support your dreams.

Manifesting
BY
Purpose

Believe IN THE Impossible

This section includes powerful exercises designed to help you manifest in specific areas, such as love, abundance, career, and success. The key to manifesting like a pro is alignment: getting your thoughts, emotions, and actions all in sync with your deepest desires. By approaching these exercises with focus and consistency, you'll tap into your own unique magic and unlock the universe's limitless potential.

Manifest Love and Self-Love

Love is something we all crave, whether it's a romantic partner, deeper bonds with loved ones, or just a stronger sense of self-love. The exercises in this section will help you open your heart and invite in the love you deserve.

Manifesting true love isn't about finding that "perfect" person; it's about cultivating a radiant energy of self-love that attracts a partner who truly vibes with you and adds to your already amazing life. When you love and accept yourself, flaws and all, you project a confidence that signals to the universe (and potential partners) that you're ready for a real, deep connection. You become a love magnet because you're already overflowing with love from within. Self-love helps you let go of past baggage and limiting beliefs about love. When you love yourself, you stop chasing after love and can focus on living your best life, and love finds its way to you.

MY MANIFESTING LOVE STORY
There was a time when my heart ached for a love that felt true and lasting. I had been on countless dates, tried online dating, and even ventured into the social scene with my friends, hoping to stumble upon "the one." But each attempt left me feeling

empty and disheartened. One evening, a wave of clarity washed over me. I realized that I had been desperately trying to control the process and force the universe to deliver my soulmate on my timeline. At that moment, I made a conscious decision to surrender.

Three months later, out of the blue, I received a message from an amazing guy who wanted me to design a tattoo for him. We started chatting, and we soon realized something incredible: we had crossed paths countless times throughout the years without ever knowing how close we were. It was as if the universe orchestrating our meeting all along. When we finally met in person, it felt like a reunion of old souls. We had so much in common, and a connection that felt both familiar and exhilarating. It was a love that surpassed anything I had ever experienced, and a love that felt destined.

My story is a testament to the power of trust and surrender. By letting go of control and focusing on my own growth and happiness, I created space for the universe to deliver my soulmate in its own perfect timing.

THE LOVE LETTER METHOD

The love letter method is a unique and powerful way to attract love. Instead of relying on traditional dating websites or apps, this technique involves writing a heartfelt letter from the perspective of your ideal partner.

In this letter, your ideal partner describes the qualities they admire in you, painting a vivid picture of your shared future and the love that binds you together.

This creative visualization, captured on paper, serves as a powerful tool in manifesting the love you desire, bringing you one step closer to your soulmate.

You will need a piece of paper and a pen for this exercise.

1| At the top of your piece of paper, address the letter to yourself. This might feel unusual, but try to trust the process.

2| Imagine your ideal partner. What are their qualities? How do they make you feel? Do you already have a specific person in mind?

3| Now, you are going to pretend you are your ideal person. Write to yourself from their eyes, expressing their admiration for you. Mention the things they love about your personality, your quirks, and your strengths. Be specific! Don't just say "you're kind;" mention a specific example of how you show kindness. Focus on the present, so instead of saying "I can't wait to meet you," write about how amazing it is to be with you now.

4| Reread and revise. Polish and rewrite the letter until it feels true and resonates with you.

THE WHISPER METHOD

The whisper method involves creating an intimate, dreamlike connection with your ideal partner. Picture them close, as if you're sharing a secret, and whisper your deepest desires directly into their ear. These desires could be anything from shared laughter to passionate adventures, or the simple yearning for a love that feels like coming home.

By whispering your longings with sincerity and visualization, you send a powerful, personalized message to the universe, attracting love that resonates with your deepest longings.

1| Imagine the person you desire a connection with. Visualize them, their surroundings, and their expression clearly.

2| See yourself approaching them with confidence.

3| Lean in and whisper your desire three times. Phrase it clearly and directly, focusing on what you want them to do or say. For example, "You message me tonight asking to hang out." While whispering, focus on the positive emotions you desire. Feel the joy of connection, the excitement of possibility, or the security of knowing they feel the same way.

4| After whispering, step back and smile. Imagine them reacting positively to your desire. Then, let it go and trust that the universe is working its magic.

MANIFESTING BY PURPOSE

FUTURE LOVE TIME CAPSULE MANIFESTATION

A love time capsule is a beautiful and creative way to actively manifest love in your life. By crafting this personalized treasure trove, you'll focus your intentions, send a powerful message to the universe, and create a tangible reminder of the love you desire.

As you seal the capsule with an affirmation of openness and trust, you'll set the stage for a beautiful unfolding of love, trusting in the universe's perfect timing.

You will need three pieces of paper and a pen; small items that represent love; your favorite perfume/cologne (optional); collaging materials; something to act as your time capsule, like a box, a jar, or a chest; and a sticky label (optional).

1| On your piece of paper, write a letter to your future love. Pour your heart out and describe the qualities you desire in a partner, your hopes and dreams for the relationship, and the kind of love you wish to experience.

2| Be specific! Don't just say "kind and funny;" elaborate on what "kind" and "funny" mean to you. Express your own wonderful qualities and let your future love know what makes you an amazing partner.

3| Once you've finished your letter, take a separate piece of paper and write down hobbies, activities, or interests you'd love to share with your future partner. This sparks connection and highlights the potential for a fulfilling relationship.

4| Collect any small items that you'd like to seal within your time capsule. These things should represent love, partnership, or qualities you desire in a relationship, and can be anything from a pair of hearts to a puzzle piece (representing finding your perfect match) or a symbol of a specific shared interest. You can also include a small vial of your favorite perfume/cologne or a handwritten note with a song lyric that resonates with your idea of love. These sensory elements can spark emotional connections when you revisit the capsule in the future.

5| To help further visualize your relationship, create a collage or drawing that visually represents your ideal love life. Include places you'd love to travel together, activities you'd enjoy, or anything that captures the essence of the love you desire.

6| When you're ready to seal your capsule, write an affirmation on the outside of the capsule (or on a sticky label), such as "I am open to receiving love that is fulfilling and abundant" or "True love is on its way to me."

7| Seal your capsule. You don't have to seal it with anything special; you can simply seal it with super glue or wax, or simply closing the lid will work just fine.

8| Decide where will you keep your time capsule. You may like to bury it for a future discovery or keep it close for regular reflection.

9| Choose when you'd like to open it and set a reminder if necessary. You may like to open it in a year, on a special occasion, or whenever you need a dose of inspiration and reflection.

THE SELF-LOVE DATE RITUAL

Regular self-love dates are like watering the plants of your soul—they nourish your self-worth and remind you that you're a priority. When you take time to focus on your wins and all the amazing things about you, your confidence gets a serious boost. This ritual is all about celebrating YOU and showering yourself with the love and attention you deserve.

Plus, those solo adventures give you a chance to check in with yourself, process your feelings, and really get to know who you are.

You will need a piece of paper and a pen for this exercise.

1| Just like you'd plan a date with someone special, block off time in your calendar for a solo adventure. Whether it's a weekly coffee date, losing yourself in a good book, a monthly spa day, or even a spontaneous afternoon outing, make it a nonnegotiable part of your routine.

2| During your self-love date, put away your phone and other distractions. Be fully present in the moment, savoring every experience and sensation. Pay attention to your thoughts and feelings, and allow yourself to simply be.

3| Take this time to reflect on your positive qualities, accomplishments, and everything you appreciate about yourself. Remind yourself of your strengths, resilience, and unique gifts, and express gratitude for all that you are.

THE MIRROR WORK FOR LOVE METHOD

Forget chasing love externally; this exercise empowers you to cultivate the inner radiance that attracts love naturally.

By transforming your relationship with yourself, you become a magnet for healthy and fulfilling connections. Feel the warmth of self-acceptance and the glow of confidence radiating from within and know that as you embody these affirmations, you'll cultivate a magnetic energy that naturally draws loving relationships into your life.

You will need a mirror for this exercise.

1| Stand in front of a mirror and look yourself in the eye. Maintain good posture and radiate confidence.

2| Instead of focusing on attracting someone, speak affirmations about your own lovability. Repeat affirmations like "I am worthy of love," "I am a loving and compassionate person," or "I radiate love and attract healthy relationships."

3| As you say these affirmations, feel the emotions associated with being loved and loving someone else.

AFFIRMATIONS FOR ATTRACTING LOVE

Everything I desire is magnetically drawn to me.

My presence is a gift and a source of joy and inspiration.

My energy is radiant and captivating, drawing others toward me.

My self-love is a beacon, illuminating my path and attracting more love into my life.

I am a channel for unconditional love, both giving and receiving it freely.

I am worthy of a love that is deep, passionate, and fulfilling.

My heart is open and receptive to the love that awaits me.

I am confident and secure in my own skin, radiating self-love and acceptance.

I release any past hurts and embrace the healing power of forgiveness.

I am surrounded by love in all its forms.

My relationships are built on trust, respect, and mutual admiration.

I am grateful for the love I have in my life and the love that is on its way.

I am a magnet for healthy, happy, and fulfilling relationships.

I am creating a life filled with love, laughter, and deep connection.

I am ready to receive the love I deserve, and I welcome it with open arms.

I communicate openly and honestly with those I love.

I am grateful for the connections I have in my life.

I am creating a community of love and support around me.

Manifest Money and Abundance

Money can be a stressor. It's easy to get caught up in feeling like there's never enough or that it's always a struggle. But what if we flipped the script? What if we started seeing money as a powerful form of energy, something we can work with instead of against?

In this section, we're going to dive into your relationship with money and see how we can shift it toward one of abundance and prosperity. We'll explore mindset shifts that can open you up to receiving more, practical exercises to help you attract financial blessings, and the magic of setting clear intentions for your financial goals.

Get ready to discover a whole new perspective on money, one where it flows to you effortlessly and joyfully. It's time to step into a reality where you're not just chasing money, but where money is chasing you.

MY GRATEFUL MONEY MANIFESTATION

I vividly remember a time when money felt tight. It was a period of uncertainty, and every bill that arrived seemed to amplify my anxieties. Then, a wise mentor shared a simple yet powerful

practice with me: the "Thank You Money" method. He instructed me to take out the cash from my wallet at the end of each day, no matter how little or how much I had. He said to sort it into piles and, with each bill I held, to whisper, "Thank you, thank you, thank you." He emphasized expressing gratitude not just for the money itself, but for the opportunities it represented, such as the ability to put food on the table, pay my rent, and even enjoy small luxuries.

As I followed his guidance, something incredible happened. My mindset shifted from one of scarcity to one of abundance. Slowly, I started noticing more opportunities for abundance. New clients seemed to appear out of thin air, and my overall financial situation began to improve. It was as if the universe was responding to my gratitude.

This experience taught me that gratitude isn't just about being polite. It's a powerful energetic force that opens the door to greater abundance. By acknowledging and appreciating the money I already had, I created a vibrational match for even more financial blessings to flow my way.

THE 369 MONEY MANIFESTING EXERCISE

This exercise combines the power of intention, repetition, and visualization to attract abundance into your life. The 369 method, popularized by Nikola Tesla, is believed to amplify the energy behind your desires.

You will need a piece of paper and a pen for this exercise.

1| Begin by getting clear on the specific amount of money you wish to manifest. Be realistic, but also allow yourself to dream big. Then, write down your desired amount in your journal. For example, "I am manifesting $5,000."

2| Turn your intention into a positive affirmation. Make it present tense and personal. For example, "I am grateful to receive $5,000."

3| As soon as you wake up, write your affirmation three times in your journal. Focus on the feeling of already having the money. Visualize how it will feel to have it in your possession and what you will do with it.

4| Connect with the emotions associated with having the money. The stronger the feeling, the more powerful your manifestation.

5| Find a quiet moment in the afternoon to write your affirmation six times in your journal. Again, focus on the feeling of abundance and visualize your desired outcome.

6| Before bed, write your affirmation nine times in your journal. Express gratitude for its arrival and visualize how it will positively impact your life.

7| Continue this practice for at least twenty-one days, as consistency is key to manifesting your desires. Have unwavering faith that your manifestation is on its way. Doubt and fear can block the flow of abundance.

THE ABUNDANCE CHECK EXERCISE

This exercise is a powerful way to attract more money into your life, as it combines intention-setting and visualization with the physical act of writing a check to yourself, helping you create a clear picture of your financial goals. By engaging both your conscious and subconscious mind, this practice can shift your mindset toward abundance, dissolve limiting beliefs, and open you up to receiving the wealth you desire.

You will need a blank check (or you can create one on a piece of paper) and a pen.

1| On the date line of the check, write the date you believe you will receive the money. This could be a specific date or simply "Now" if you want to manifest it immediately.

2| In the "Pay to the order of" line, write your full name.

3| In the numerical box on the check, write the exact amount of money you wish to manifest.

4| On the line below "Pay to the order of," write out the amount in words. For example, if you wrote $10,000 in the box, write "Ten Thousand Dollars" on the line.

5| In the memo line, write "For Abundant Wealth" or another positive affirmation that resonates with you. Then, sign the check as if you were the universe or your higher self.

6| Put the check in a safe place where you will see it often. You can also carry it with you in your wallet or purse.

7| Each time you see the check, visualize yourself receiving the money and feel the emotions associated with having it. Imagine how it will feel to have that money in your possession and what you will do with it.

8| Express gratitude for the money as if you have already received it, as gratitude opens the door for more abundance to flow into your life.

9| Continue to take inspired action toward your financial goals. The universe rewards those who take initiative.

10| Let go of any attachment to the outcome. Trust that the universe will deliver in the perfect way and timing.

The Money Magnet Meditation

This money magnet meditation is a powerful visualization exercise designed to help you attract wealth and prosperity into your life. By harnessing the power of your mind and focusing your intention, you can develop a magnetic energy that draws money toward you effortlessly.

This simple yet effective practice can shift your mindset, dissolve any blocks to abundance, and open you up to receiving the financial blessings you deserve.

1| Find a comfortable and quiet place where you won't be disturbed. Sit or lie down in a relaxed position.

2| Close your eyes and take several deep breaths, inhaling slowly through your nose and exhaling through your mouth. Feel your body relax more and more with each breath.

3| Imagine that you have a powerful magnet in the center of your chest, pulling money and abundance toward you. See the magnet glowing brightly and feel its magnetic force attracting wealth from all directions.

4| Visualize money flowing toward you in various forms—cash, checks, online payments, unexpected gifts. See it coming to you easily and effortlessly.

5 | As you visualize the money flowing in, feel a sense of deep gratitude for this abundance.

6 | If affirmations resonate with you, you can silently repeat positive statements, such as "I am a money magnet," "Money flows to me easily and abundantly," or "I am grateful for all the wealth in my life."

7 | Continue to breathe deeply and visualize for 5–10 minutes.

8 | When you're ready, gently open your eyes and take a few moments to ground yourself back in the present moment.

THE DECLUTTERING METHOD

Manifesting your dream life starts with aligning your energy with its abundance. Decluttering is a powerful tool to achieve this, creating both physical and energetic space for your new life to come into being. Decluttering also unlocks the doorway to abundance.

By letting go of possessions that no longer spark joy or serve a purpose, you're making space—physically and energetically—for things that truly resonate with your dreams and goals. This act of releasing aligns your vibration with the abundant flow of the universe, attracting more of what you truly desire into your life.

You will need storage containers or boxes (optional) for this exercise.

1| Set aside some time to fully commit to this exercise, and identify an area or areas that you want to declutter, like your home or workspace.

2| Begin your declutter by setting an intention to work slowly, calmly, and mindfully.

3| Have some boxes or bags close at hand as you begin to declutter. As you tidy and sort through any clutter, ask yourself: Does this item spark joy? Does it serve a purpose in my life currently? Does it align with the vision of my dream life? Be honest with yourself. If the answer is no, thank the item for its service and put it in a "let go of" pile.

4| As you declutter, focus on the abundance and visualize the space you're creating for your dream life. Imagine the joy of filling it with items you truly love and that resonate with your vision.

5| Once you've decluttered, organize your "let go of" pile into things you can donate or recycle, sorting items into categories like clothes, books, or electronics, giving thanks and gratitude for the abundance you already have. Donate quality, gently used items to charities or shelters to give them a new life and send positive energy out into the universe.

6| When you're ready to finish, take a moment to appreciate the fresh, open space you've created. This is more than just physical—it's also an energetic shift. You've made room for new possibilities to flow into your life.

AFFIRMATIONS FOR ATTRACTING MONEY AND ABUNDANCE

I am financially free and abundant.

I effortlessly attract wealth and prosperity.

I live a life of luxury and comfort.

I am blessed beyond measure.

My luck and blessings multiply with every passing moment.

I am a magnet for good fortune and serendipity.

The universe conspires in my favor, opening doors of opportunity.

I am in the right place at the right time.

I see possibilities everywhere I look.

I embrace challenges as stepping-stones to success.

I trust my intuition to guide me toward the best opportunities.

I am living a life of endless possibilities.

I am worthy of all the good that comes my way.

I am open to receiving unexpected blessings.

I am grateful for the abundance that surrounds me.

Every day brings new opportunities for growth and success.

Manifest Career Success

Career success isn't just about a fat paycheck. It's about finding work that lights you up, uses your unique talents, and makes you feel like you're contributing something meaningful to the world. In this section, we'll dive into exercises designed to help you manifest your dream career, whether that's landing the perfect job, launching your own successful business, or reigniting a passion for what you're already doing.

These practices will empower you to take inspired action and create opportunities you might not have even imagined. Get ready to unleash your full potential and build a career that brings you joy, abundance, and a deep sense of satisfaction.

HOW I MANIFESTED ONE OF MY DREAM CAREERS
There was a time in my life when I felt unfulfilled as a stay-at-home mom, longing for a creative outlet and a sense of financial independence. Then, an unexpected opportunity presented itself. A local tattoo shop I often visited was looking for a dedicated body piercer. Despite having no experience, a persistent voice inside me whispered, "Why not? What's the worst that could happen? No?" Trusting that inner nudge, I

decided to take a chance. I reached out to the shop, expressing my connection and my willingness to learn. To my surprise and delight, they offered me the opportunity to train as a body piercer.

A year later, a new path opened up. Artists I admired began suggesting I consider a tattoo apprenticeship, recognizing the dedication I poured into honing my drawing skills. Once again, I listened to my gut and took another leap, pouring my heart into the apprenticeship. Looking back, I realize that my journey as a tattoo artist wasn't just about acquiring a new skill; it was about trusting my intuition and taking inspired action. It was about recognizing the subtle nudges from the universe and having the courage to follow them, even when the path seemed uncertain.

By honoring my authentic self and embracing opportunities, I transformed my life. And that's the beauty of manifestation. It's not just about achieving your dreams; it's about discovering the limitless potential that lies within you.

THE TALK SHOW EXERCISE

Like any skill, manifestation takes practice. By repeating this exercise, you'll begin to refine your vision and strengthen your connection to your dream career.

This method combines visualization and emotional embodiment to create a powerful manifesting experience. By feeling and acting "as if" you already have your dream job, you program your subconscious mind and radiate an energy that can attract opportunities that align with your desires.

1 Find a quiet space where you won't be interrupted.

2 Picture a friendly talk show host interviewing you. Give them a name and personality to make it more real.

3 Respond to their questions about your dream job with enthusiasm and confidence. Example questions could include:

- ✦ What sparked your interest in this field?
- ✦ When did you first realize this was the career path for you?
- ✦ Walk us through a typical day in your dream job.
- ✦ What's the most exciting part of your job? What gets you out of bed in the morning?
- ✦ What skills or qualities are essential for success in this field?
- ✦ What's the most rewarding aspect of your dream job? What gives you the most satisfaction?

✦ How does your work contribute to the world or make a positive impact?

✦ What advice would you give to someone who aspires to have a similar career?

4| Talk about how grateful you are to be in this role and how it allows you to utilize your skills and make a positive impact. As you answer the questions, pay close attention to how you feel. Imagine the joy, fulfillment, and sense of accomplishment that come with your dream job.

5| Immerse yourself in the positive emotions associated with your success. Let the feeling of having your dream job wash over you.

6| Conduct these "talk shows" regularly. The more you practice, the more vivid and powerful the experience will become. Over time, you'll refine your answers and delve deeper into the details of your dream job.

THE ACT AS IF METHOD

This method is based on the idea that by embodying the person you want to become, you signal to the universe (and yourself) that you're ready for that reality. Inspired action takes many forms, and sometimes it starts with simply "acting as if."

By embodying the qualities and habits of your dream career in your day-to-day life using the points below, you'll send a powerful message to the universe (and yourself) that you're ready for that reality.

1| Wherever you work from, start incorporating elements of your desired career wardrobe into your daily attire. Feeling confident and professional can boost your energy and self-belief. It can also signal to others how you see yourself and the professional you want to be.

2| Pay attention to the terminology used in your desired field. Start incorporating it into your daily conversations, even if it feels awkward at first. Speaking the language of success can influence your mindset and attract opportunities.

3| Identify someone who embodies the career you desire. Observe their habits, communication style, and approach to work. Try incorporating some of these elements into your own routine, as this allows you to "test-drive" the career and see how it fits with your personality and goals.

4| Attend industry events, connect with people on professional networking sites, and actively engage in discussions related to your field. Build relationships with individuals already in your desired career. These connections can offer valuable insights and potential opportunities.

5| Invest time in acquiring the skills and knowledge necessary for your dream career. Take online courses, attend workshops, read industry publications, and actively seek opportunities to apply your learning. This demonstrates your commitment to professional growth and makes you a more attractive candidate.

6| Create a workspace that inspires and motivates you. If you're working from home, designate a specific area solely for work. Personalize your workspace with items that remind you of your career goals and create a sense of professionalism.

7| Commit to constantly expanding your knowledge and skills. Read books, listen to podcasts, and attend seminars related to your industry. The more you know, the more confident you'll feel and the more prepared you'll be for opportunities when they arise.

LIVING THE DREAM JOURNAL

Imagine stepping into your ideal career, feeling the excitement and fulfillment of doing work you love. This exercise invites you to make that vision a reality.

By consistently writing about your day as if you're already living your dream job, you'll harness the power of manifestation, aligning your energy with your desires and attracting your ideal career into your life.

You will need a journal and a pen for this exercise. Select a journal that inspires you. It could be a physical notebook, a digital document, or even a dedicated app.

1| Each day, set aside time to write in your journal as if you're already working in your dream job. Use these prompts to guide your writing and bring your dream job to life, writing in the present tense:

- ✦ "Today at work, I. . .": Describe the tasks and projects you tackled.
- ✦ "I felt energized when. . .": Highlight the moments that brought you joy and excitement.
- ✦ "I collaborated with. . .": Write about the interactions you had with colleagues and clients.
- ✦ "I am grateful for. . .": Express appreciation for the opportunities and experiences your dream job provides.
- ✦ "I celebrated my success by. . .": Describe how you acknowledge each of your achievements and milestones.

2| Make your entries as vivid as possible by including sensory details. What did you see, hear, smell, taste, and touch during your workday? The more specific and detailed your entries, the more real your dream job will feel.

3| Describe the emotions you experienced throughout the day. How did your dream job make you feel?

4| Regularly review your journal entries to immerse yourself in the experience of living your dream job. Pay attention to the recurring themes and emotions that arise.

AFFIRMATIONS FOR ATTRACTING CAREER SUCCESS

I am a highly skilled and experienced professional, perfectly suited for my dream job at [company name].

My knowledge and expertise are valuable assets that will contribute significantly to [desired company/role].

I am constantly learning and growing, developing the skills needed to excel in my dream career.

I am confident and prepared to take on the challenges and responsibilities of my dream job.

I am a determined and motivated individual with a proven track record of success.

I am worthy of achieving my dream job
and attracting opportunities that
align with my goals.

I am creative and inspired.

My ideas flow freely and effortlessly.

I express myself with authenticity and joy.

I am open to new ideas and possibilities.

I am grateful for the creative
spark within me.

Manifest Health and Wellness

Your body is a masterpiece, a symphony of cells and energy, constantly responding to the signals your mind sends its way. The mind-body connection is a powerful one, and one that can either uplift or hold you back. If you're stuck in a loop of negative self-talk or limiting beliefs about your health, your body is listening.

But what if you could train your brain to become your biggest cheerleader, flooding your cells with messages of positivity, healing, and vitality? That's the essence of manifesting health and wellness. It's not just about the external actions you take; it's about transforming your thoughts and beliefs to create a ripple effect of well-being that radiates from the inside out. The exercises in this section will guide you through powerful techniques to harness the connection between your mind and body, empowering you to manifest vibrant health and lasting well-being.

MY JOURNEY TO HEALTH AND WELLNESS

I used to take my health for granted, but then a series of unexpected health challenges threw me completely off balance. After a battery of tests and a hefty doctor's bill, the verdict

was... anticlimactic. "Maybe it's stress?" the doctor suggested. I felt like modern medicine had failed me, and I realized I needed to become my own advocate to reclaim my health.

I'd already been practicing manifestation and had seen some amazing results in other areas of my life, but I'd never thought to apply it to my health. But facing this health crisis, I realized it was time to change that. I started small, and began a gratitude practice, focusing on the parts of my body that were functioning well. I visualized myself radiating energy and vitality, and I even created a vision board filled with images of nourishing foods.

Slowly but surely, something started to shift. I began making healthier choices out of a genuine desire to nurture my body. I started listening to my intuition, tuning in to what my body needed. The journey wasn't linear, and there were days when the fatigue crept back in, or a new symptom would appear out of nowhere. But I kept taking inspired action. And then, something amazing happened. I felt more alive, more vibrant, and more connected to my body than ever before.

THE HEALTHY HABITS RITUAL

Healthy habits are the key to feeling amazing, but sometimes they can feel tough. This exercise is all about flipping the script and turning healthy choices into something you actually look forward to, a sacred ritual that nourishes your mind, body, and soul.

You will need a lighter or matches, a candle, soothing music, and essential oils to diffuse (optional) for this exercise.

1| Think of a few healthy habits you want to improve. Perhaps drinking more water, exercising regularly, or sleeping well. Choose habits that align with your wellness goals and genuinely excite you.

2| Set aside a special spot in your home or a specific time of day for your healthy habit ritual. This helps you create intention and prioritize these actions amid the busyness.

3| Connect each habit to a deeper purpose. If you're drinking more water, visualize it cleansing and energizing your cells. If you're exercising, imagine yourself getting stronger with every move.

4| Make your ritual a full-on sensory experience. Light a candle, play some chill music, or diffuse essential oils to create a peaceful and inviting atmosphere.

5| As you engage in your healthy habit, take a moment to appreciate your amazing body and its ability to heal and thrive. Gratitude is a powerful energy booster!

Example Rituals to Inspire You

When you prioritize activities that nourish you, your whole vibe starts to shift. You radiate positivity, and that attracts even more good things into your life. It's also a chance to really tune in to your body and what it needs. That mind-body connection is crucial, and the more you understand yourself, the easier it is to make choices that truly support your well-being.

MORNING HYDRATION RITUAL

Kick-start your day with a warm cup of lemon water, visualizing it revitalizing your system. Take a few moments to bask in the feeling of hydration and set a positive intention for the day ahead.

MINDFUL MOVEMENT RITUAL

Wind down each evening with 30 minutes of gentle yoga or a peaceful walk in nature. Focus on your breath, the sensations in your body, and the pure joy of movement.

NOURISHING BEDTIME RITUAL

Create a cozy bedtime routine with a few pages of an inspiring book, a cup of chamomile tea, and the calming scent of lavender. Visualize yourself drifting off to a peaceful sleep, allowing your body to fully recharge.

THE BODY GRATITUDE RITUAL

This ritual is designed to help you cultivate a deep appreciation for your body (your home) and all that it does for you. By focusing on gratitude for your physical vessel, you can shift your energy toward self-love, healing, and well-being.

You will need a lighter or matches, a candle, soothing music, and essential oils to diffuse (optional) for this exercise.

1| Find a quiet and comfortable space where you can relax and connect with your body. Light a candle, play soothing music, or diffuse essential oils to enhance the ambience.

2| Close your eyes and take a few deep breaths, bringing your awareness to the present moment. Feel the rise and fall of your chest as you inhale and exhale, and notice the sensation of the air entering and leaving your body.

3| Begin by expressing gratitude for your body. Appreciate its strength, resilience, and ability to support you through life's journey. Thank your body for all that it does for you, from carrying you through your day to allowing you to experience the world through your senses.

4| Now, bring your attention to specific parts of your body, starting from your head and moving down to your toes. Express gratitude for each part and its unique function. Here are some examples that you can use, but feel free to add to this or modify:

- ✦ **Head:** Thank your head for housing your brain, your senses, and your beautiful thoughts and ideas.
- ✦ **Eyes:** Appreciate your eyes for allowing you to see the world in all its beauty.
- ✦ **Ears:** Express gratitude for your ears, which enable you to hear music, laughter, and the voices of those you care about.
- ✦ **Nose:** Thank your nose for allowing you to smell the sweet fragrance of flowers, the delicious aroma of your favorite meal, and the comforting scent of home.
- ✦ **Mouth:** Appreciate your mouth for allowing you to taste delicious food, express yourself through words, and share smiles and laughter.
- ✦ **Heart:** Thank your heart for pumping life-giving blood throughout your body and for holding your capacity for love and compassion.
- ✦ **Lungs:** Express gratitude for your lungs, which allow you to breathe and experience the vital energy of life.
- ✦ **Stomach:** Appreciate your stomach for digesting the food that nourishes you and providing energy for your daily activities.
- ✦ **Legs and feet:** Thank your legs and feet for carrying you through life's adventures, allowing you to explore the world and connect with nature.

As you express gratitude for each part of your body, visualize sending love and appreciation to that area.

5| Once you've completed your body scan, take a few more deep breaths and express gratitude for the overall health and well-being you experience.

6| Practice this exercise daily, weekly, or whenever you feel the need to connect with your body and develop self-love.

THE RECIPE ADVENTURE

Food is more than just fuel; it's a source of pleasure, nourishment, and a way to connect with yourself and the world around you.

This exercise empowers you to tap into that power and create a vibrant, joyful relationship with food. Say goodbye to restrictive diets and hello to a world of delicious, nourishing ingredients that support your well-being and make you feel amazing. It's time to unleash your inner foodie and manifest a life filled with health, happiness, and culinary delights.

1| Each week, embark on a culinary quest to discover a new healthy recipe that sparks your curiosity and aligns with your wellness goals. Think of it as a treasure hunt for deliciousness and vitality. Browse cookbooks, scroll through food blogs, or get recommendations from friends and health experts.

2| Turn cooking into a fun and mindful experience. Invite loved ones to join you, put on some upbeat music, and let your inner chef shine. Experiment with different ingredients, flavors, and presentation styles. As you prepare your meal, infuse it with positive intentions for health.

3| When it's time to eat, slow down and savor each bite mindfully. Pay attention to the textures, flavors, and aromas. Notice how it makes you feel, and express gratitude for the nourishment and positive energy it's bringing to your body and life.

THE MINDFUL GROCERY SHOPPING EXERCISE

Your kitchen is a reflection of your wellness journey, so let's make it a beautiful one. Mindful grocery shopping goes beyond simply buying food; it's about intentionally choosing ingredients that nourish your body and align with your highest vision for yourself.

When you stock up on healthy goodies, you're basically setting yourself up for success, as it's much easier to make nourishing choices when tempting snacks aren't constantly calling your name. Plus, you're taking control of your health journey and making conscious choices that align with your goals, which is incredibly empowering.

1| Before heading to the store, take a moment to connect with your wellness vision. What kind of foods will support your goals? What will make you feel energized and vibrant? Write a list of healthy options that align with your intentions.

2| As you browse the aisles, be mindful of your choices. Focus on whole, unprocessed foods that come from the earth. Choose vibrant fruits and vegetables, lean proteins, healthy fats, and whole grains. Stick to your list and avoid impulse purchases. Remember, you're in control of what you buy.

3| Take a moment to appreciate the abundance of healthy options available to you. Express gratitude for the farmers, producers, and everyone involved in bringing nourishing food to your table.

AFFIRMATIONS FOR ATTRACTING HEALTH AND WELLNESS

I am vibrant, healthy, and full of energy.

My body is strong, flexible, and resilient.

I radiate inner peace and happiness.

I nourish my body with healthy food and exercise.

I listen to my body's wisdom and honor its needs.

I am grateful for my physical health and well-being.

I am creating a life filled with vitality and energy.

I am committed to taking care of my physical and mental health.

I am at peace with my body and love
it unconditionally.

My body is a temple, and I treat it
with respect and care.

I am filled with energy and
enthusiasm for life.

I am embracing a healthy
and active lifestyle.

I am grateful for the ability to move
my body freely.

I am creating a life of balance
and harmony.

I am radiating health and vitality
from the inside out.

Manifest Purpose and Fulfillment

Feeling good is fantastic, but there's more to life than just feeling good, right? It's time to tap into something deeper, something that truly sets your soul on fire. In this section, we're diving into the juicy realm of purpose and fulfillment.

Think of it like this: you've built a solid foundation of well-being. Now, it's time to design and build the life of your dreams on top of that foundation. What are you truly passionate about? What makes you feel alive? What kind of impact do you want to make on the world? This is a journey of self-discovery, where you'll unlock your true potential and create a life that's bursting with purpose and meaning. It's time to unleash your inner superstar and shine!

FINDING MY PURPOSE IN SHARING THE MAGIC

My journey to purpose and fulfillment wasn't a straight line; it was more like a winding path through an enchanted forest, full of unexpected twists and turns. For years, I chased the dream of becoming a renowned tattoo artist. I honed my craft, built a loyal clientele, and even had the opportunity to tattoo some well-known celebrities. It was the life I'd always envisioned for

myself, and yet, despite achieving this long-held goal, a nagging sense of emptiness lingered.

The truth was that the day-to-day reality of the work started to feel limiting. I yearned for something more. I wanted to make a greater impact and empower others on a broader scale.

The turning point came unexpectedly during a quiet moment of reflection. I realized that the joy I felt wasn't just in the act of creating art, but in witnessing the transformation my clients underwent. From that moment, I began to see my skills and experiences not just as tools for creating art, but as a means to inspire and guide others on their own paths. I started exploring new avenues for sharing my knowledge, growing my social media platform, where I connected with individuals seeking personal growth and transformation.

Today, I dedicate my life to empowering others through writing, teaching, and sharing my story, and the sense of fulfillment I feel is beyond anything I could have imagined in my previous life.

THE SOUL'S CALLING JOURNALING EXERCISE

Ever feel like there's something more you're meant to be doing? A deeper purpose waiting to be discovered?

This journaling exercise is your invitation to tune in to your inner wisdom and uncover those hidden passions and desires that are yearning to be expressed. By reflecting on these prompts and letting your thoughts flow freely, you'll gain valuable insights into your true self, your values, and your soul's calling.

You will need a journal and a pen for this exercise.

1| Find a cozy nook where you can relax with your journal.

2| Take a few deep breaths, allowing your mind and body to settle into a state of calm and openness. Let go of any worries or distractions and bring your focus to the present moment.

3| Now, it's time dive into some soul-searching prompts. Remember, there are no right or wrong answers here. Just be honest with yourself and let your intuition guide your words. Choose as many of the prompts below as you would like to journal about, and write your answers in your journal:

✦ What activities make me lose track of time?

✦ What am I doing when I feel most alive and in the flow?

✦ What skills and talents do I possess that bring me joy? What comes naturally to me?

✦ What do I love to do, even if I don't consider myself an "expert"?

- ✦ What impact do I want to make in the world?
- ✦ What kind of positive change do I want to see?
- ✦ How can I use my unique gifts to contribute?
- ✦ What kind of legacy do I want to leave behind?
- ✦ How do I want to be remembered?

4| Let your thoughts and feelings flow onto the page without judgment or censorship. Don't worry about grammar or perfect sentences. Just write from the heart.

5| Once you've finished journaling, take some time to reflect on your answers. What themes or patterns emerge? What insights have you gained about your passions, values, and aspirations? Use these reflections to guide you as you continue your journey of manifesting a life of purpose and fulfillment.

THE PURPOSEFUL PLAYLIST CREATION

Music has a unique way of touching our souls and inspiring us to reach for our dreams.

This exercise is all about curating a personalized soundtrack for your journey toward purpose and fulfillment. The right songs can uplift your spirit, motivate you to take action, and remind you of your deepest desires and aspirations.

1| Think about the songs that make your heart sing, the lyrics that speak to your deepest desires, and the melodies that move you to action. Choose songs that resonate with your values, dreams, and aspirations.

2| Gather your favorite songs and create a playlist that embodies your purpose and fuels your motivation.

3| Listen to your playlist while working on your goals, during moments of self-reflection, or whenever you need a boost of inspiration. Let the music remind you of your purpose and ignite your passion.

THE INNER CHILD RECONNECTION

Remember that carefree, curious kid you used to be? The one who dreamed big, loved to play, and saw the world with wonder? That inner child is still a part of you, holding the keys to your true passions and purpose.

This exercise is your chance to reconnect with that playful spirit and unlock the hidden wisdom they hold. Make time for activities that bring you joy and connect you to your inner child, as even small moments of playfulness can make a big difference.

You will need a piece of paper and a pen for this exercise.

1| Find a comfortable spot where you can relax.

2| Close your eyes and take a few deep breaths. Imagine yourself as that younger version of you, full of dreams and possibilities. What activities did you love most? What made your heart sing? What did you dream of becoming? Let those memories come flooding back.

3| Now, grab a pen and paper and write a letter to your inner child. Tell them about their dreams, their passions, and their boundless imagination. Express your love and appreciation for them, and let them know that you're committed to honoring their spirit in your adult life.

4| Take a look at those childhood passions and dreams. How can you bring a little bit of that magic into your life today? Find ways to sprinkle that childlike wonder and joy back into your everyday life.

The Purposeful Pause Meditation

In the whirlwind of everyday life, it's easy to lose touch with our deeper purpose and passions. This purposeful pause meditation is your invitation to hit the pause button, quiet the noise, and create space for stillness and reflection. It's a chance to connect with your inner wisdom and tap into the whispers of your soul, guiding you toward a life filled with meaning and fulfillment.

You will need a lighter or matches (optional), a candle (optional), a timer, and a piece of paper and a pen for this exercise.

1| Find a quiet and comfy spot where you won't be interrupted. Dim the lights, light a candle, or do whatever helps you create a peaceful atmosphere.

2| Set a timer for 5-10 minutes to begin with. As you get more comfortable with meditation, you can gradually increase the duration.

3| Close your eyes, take a few deep breaths, and let your body relax. Focus on the sensation of your breath moving in and out, anchoring you to the present moment.

4| Silently ask yourself: What is my purpose? What brings me the most joy and fulfillment? Don't try to force an answer. Just hold the questions in your mind and see what arises.

5| Thoughts, feelings, images, or even just sensations might come up. Don't judge them or try to analyze them. Simply observe them with curiosity and openness.

6| When your timer goes off, gently open your eyes and grab your journal.

7| Jot down any thoughts, feelings, or insights that surfaced during your meditation. These could be valuable clues to your deeper purpose and passions.

AFFIRMATIONS FOR ATTRACTING CONFIDENCE AND SELF-ESTEEM

I am vibrant, healthy, and full of energy.

I am confident and capable.

I believe in myself and my abilities.

I am worthy of success and happiness.

I trust my intuition and make decisions with clarity.

I am strong, resilient, and full of potential.

I am proud of myself and my accomplishments.

I am comfortable in my own skin.

I am deserving of love and respect.

I radiate confidence and inner strength.

I am embracing my authentic self.

I am overcoming challenges and growing stronger each day.

I am attracting positive relationships and experiences.

I am creating a life I love.

I am grateful for all that I am.

I am worthy of all good things.

Manifest Confidence and Self-Esteem

Ever feel like self-doubt is holding you back from truly living your best life? Or like there's a more confident, empowered version of you just waiting to break free?

Developing confidence and self-esteem is absolutely crucial for creating a life filled with joy, success, and fulfillment.

When you believe in yourself and your worth, you radiate a magnetic energy that attracts opportunities, empowers you to take risks, and helps you navigate challenges with grace and resilience.

The exercises in this section are designed to help you silence your inner critic, reprogram your mindset for success, and cultivate a deep sense of self-confidence.

MY JOURNEY TO CONFIDENCE AND SELF-BELIEF
Growing up, I was basically invisible. Shy, awkward, and super self-conscious, I blended into the background like I was wearing camouflage. I had a few people I knew, but zero real friends, and my social life was nonexistent. My lack of confidence made me doubt myself and feel like I wasn't good enough.

I desperately wanted to feel confident, to own my space, and to speak my mind without worrying about what people thought, so I decided to take charge. I started small, with daily affirmations. I'd look in the mirror and repeat things such as, "I am confident" or "I deserve good things." At first, it felt like I was trying to trick myself. But slowly, things started to change.
I started noticing that inner voice that was always putting me down, and I began to challenge negative thoughts. I started hyping myself up instead of trash-talking myself, and I celebrated every little win, no matter how small. Day by day, I felt a shift. The more I focused on what I was good at and all the cool things I had done, the more confident I became.

It wasn't always easy. There were times I doubted myself, and old insecurities would creep back in. But I kept going, reminding myself of how far I'd come. And one day, I realized I had become that confident woman I always wanted to be. I wasn't afraid of social situations anymore. I could say what I thought without overthinking it. I was no longer hiding in the shadows; I was owning my power.

THE INNER CHAMPION AFFIRMATION MIRROR RITUAL

This exercise combines the power of positive affirmations with the visual impact of seeing yourself in the mirror. Step into your inner champion and unleash a confident, radiant you.

By speaking these statements aloud and connecting with the emotions behind them, you're essentially reprogramming your subconscious mind to believe in your worth and potential. This can lead to increased self-esteem, confidence, and a more positive outlook on life.

You will need a mirror for this exercise.

MANIFESTING

1| Find a mirror where you can see your whole reflection. Take a deep breath and soften your gaze.

2| Look directly into your own eyes. This might feel awkward at first, but it's a powerful way to connect with yourself on a deeper level.

3| Start repeating affirmations that resonate with the confident, empowered version of yourself you want to become. For example, "I am confident and capable." Say them out loud, with conviction and feeling.

4| Imagine what it would be like to truly embody these qualities. Let the emotions of confidence, self-belief, and empowerment wash over you.

5| Practice this exercise daily, especially in the morning or before facing a challenging situation.

THE CELEBRATE YOUR WINS EXERCISE

Forget dwelling on what's left to do; let's celebrate how far you've come! Recognizing your accomplishments, even the seemingly insignificant ones, is like giving yourself a daily dose of self-love and appreciation, boosting your self-esteem in the process. As your list of achievements grows, you'll start to see yourself in a whole new light.

This exercise is your personal victory log, a place to track your progress and remind yourself of the awesome things you're capable of.

You will need a new journal and a pen for this exercise.

1| Acquire a journal or notebook that sparks joy and dedicate it solely to celebrating your wins. You can decorate it, add stickers to it, or make it as fancy as you want. This is your personal space to shine.

2| Each day, take a few minutes to reflect on your day and write down at least one thing you're proud of. It could be anything. Nailed a presentation at work? Write it down. Cooked a delicious and healthy meal? That's a win.

3| Make it a habit to regularly flip through your journal and relive those moments of accomplishment. By focusing on your wins, big and small, you shift your mindset from lack to abundance, creating a positive and empowering outlook.

THE CONFIDENCE-BOOSTING VISUALIZATION

Are you ready to tap into your inner strength and cultivate unwavering confidence? Visualization is a powerful technique that can reprogram your subconscious mind and help you embody the self-assured person you aspire to be.

This exercise will guide you in creating a mental image of yourself radiating confidence and achieving your goals, paving the way for that same confidence to manifest in your everyday life.

1| Settle into a quiet and comfortable space where you won't be interrupted. Close your eyes and take a few deep breaths to relax your body and mind.

2| Now, imagine yourself in a situation where you feel incredibly confident and self-assured.

3| Visualize the scene in vivid detail:

✦ How are you dressed? What's your posture like? Imagine yourself looking and feeling your best.

✦ What are you doing in this scenario? Are you speaking clearly and confidently? Are you making eye contact and engaging with others with ease? See yourself navigating the situation with grace and poise.

✦ How do you feel in this moment of confidence? Pay attention to the sensations in your body and feel them all.

4 Engage all your senses to make the visualization even more powerful:

- ✦ Imagine the sounds around you, like the hum of conversation, the applause after your presentation, or the upbeat music playing in the background.
- ✦ Feel the confidence radiating from within you. Notice the sensations of strength, clarity, and self-belief.
- ✦ Visualize the positive reactions of others. See them smiling, nodding in agreement, and being drawn to your confident energy.

5 Practice this visualization regularly, especially before situations that trigger self-doubt. The more you immerse yourself in this experience, the more your subconscious mind will start to believe it, and the more confident you'll become in real life.

AFFIRMATIONS FOR ATTRACTING CONFIDENCE AND SELF-ESTEEM

I am confident and capable.

I believe in myself and my abilities.

I am worthy of success and happiness.

I trust my intuition and make decisions with clarity.

I am strong, resilient, and full of potential.

I am proud of myself and my accomplishments.

I am comfortable in my own skin.

I am deserving of love and respect.

I radiate confidence and inner strength.

I am embracing my authentic self.

I am overcoming challenges and growing stronger each day.

I am attracting positive relationships and experiences.

I am creating a life I love.

I am grateful for all that I am.

I am worthy of all good things.

Manifest Spiritual Growth

Forget rigid rules and dogma. Manifesting spiritual growth and connection is about creating your own unique path to inner peace and fulfillment. It's about tuning into your intuition, exploring different practices, and discovering what truly resonates with your soul. It's about finding stillness amid the chaos, cultivating gratitude for the present moment, and opening yourself up to divine guidance.

Whether through meditation, nature connection, creative expression, or simply quiet contemplation, these exercises will help you deepen your spiritual connection and manifest a life filled with meaning, joy, and a profound sense of belonging in the universe.

MY SPIRITUAL MANIFESTATION JOURNEY

My spiritual journey has been a wild and wonderful ride, leading me to a deep connection with the universe and a profound sense of inner peace. Growing up, my mom encouraged exploring different spiritual beliefs. She knew true faith comes from within, and she wanted me to find my own path. This sparked a curiosity in me, a thirst for knowledge that I still have today.

For years, I dabbled in various spiritual traditions, but still felt like something was missing. Then, my sister-in-law introduced me to a whole new world of spirituality. She was passionate about meditation, energy healing, and the Law of Attraction. I was intrigued and soaked up everything she shared.

Inspired, I started meditating every day. At first, my mind would not be still. But eventually I started to experience moments of pure peace and clarity. I felt connected to something bigger than myself. I also explored other spiritual tools such as chakras and energy healing. It was like seeing the world with new eyes, recognizing the interconnectedness of everything and the infinite possibilities within me.

Through this journey, I found a sense of peace and purpose I'd never known before. I learned to trust my gut, connect with my inner wisdom, and manifest my desires with confidence.

This journey has been an amazing gift, and a reminder that spirituality is a ever-evolving and personal adventure. The most important thing is to follow your heart and trust your inner guide.

THE SOUL-NOURISHING ACTIVITIES LIST

Ever feel like you're running on autopilot, disconnected from what truly lights you up? It's time to rediscover your inner spark and prioritize activities that nourish your soul.

Taking time for activities that truly light you up is like giving your soul a much-needed recharge. It's essential for your overall well-being, helping you feel more grounded, connected, and alive. This exercise will help you identify the passions and pursuits that bring you joy, peace, and a deep sense of connection so that you can create a life that feels truly fulfilling.

You will need a piece of paper and a pen for this exercise.

1| On your piece of paper, start brainstorming a list of activities that make you feel connected, grounded, and inspired. Think about what brings you joy, peace, and a sense of wonder. Here are some ideas to get you started:

✦ Spending time in nature

✦ Mind-body practices like yoga, meditation, or breathwork

✦ Painting, writing, music, dance, or any form of self-expression

✦ Reading spiritual texts or exploring different spiritual traditions

✦ Spending quality time with loved ones or volunteering for a cause you care about

2| Once you've created your list, schedule these soul-nourishing activities into your daily or weekly routine, just like you would any other important appointment.

THE SACRED SPACE CREATION

In the midst of our busy lives, it can be easy to feel disconnected from our inner selves, yearning for a place of peace and tranquility.

This exercise invites you to transform a simple corner of your home into a sacred sanctuary—a personal haven dedicated to nurturing your spiritual well-being. This will become a space where you can escape the noise and distractions of the outside world, quiet your mind, and connect with your inner wisdom.

1| Find a quiet corner or room in your home where you won't be interrupted. It could be a spare bedroom, a cozy nook in your living room, or even a dedicated corner of your bedroom.

2| Make it your own by decorating it with items that inspire you and create a sense of peace and tranquility. This could include:

- ✦ Calming colors
- ✦ Natural elements like plants or flowers
- ✦ Soft lighting or candles
- ✦ A comfy chair or cushions
- ✦ Personal touches like photos or crystals

3| Use this space for your daily spiritual practices, whether it's meditation, prayer, journaling, or simply sitting in quiet contemplation. The more you use it, the more powerful its energy will become.

THE SPIRITUAL EXPLORATION ADVENTURE

Do you ever feel like there's more to life than meets the eye, or like there's a whole universe of spiritual wisdom and practices out there waiting to be discovered? This exercise is your invitation to embark on a journey of exploration.

Going on a spiritual journey is like opening a treasure chest full of possibilities, as it's about expanding your horizons and deepening your understanding of the universe and your place within it. It's a chance to break free from old patterns and beliefs, discover hidden strengths, and connect with your intuition on a whole new level.

1| Start by tapping into your curiosity. What spiritual traditions, philosophies, or practices intrigue you? Maybe you've always been fascinated by Buddhism, or perhaps you're drawn to the energy healing modalities like Reiki. Make a list of anything that piques your interest.

2| Once you have your list, it's time to dive in. There are endless ways to explore. You can pick up books on different traditions, philosophies, or self-development practices; explore websites, blogs, and online courses related to your areas of interest; or attend workshops, retreats, or classes to experience different practices firsthand.

3| Don't be afraid to try different techniques and see what resonates with you, paying attention to how each practice makes you feel. What brings you a sense of peace, joy, or connection?

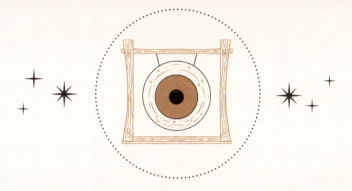

THE SACRED SOUND BATH EXPERIENCE

Sound baths are like a gentle lullaby for your brain waves, easing them into a slower, more relaxed state. The vibrations from the sounds can even help release energetic blockages and promote healing on a cellular level. It's a truly transformative experience that leaves you feeling refreshed, aligned, and connected to your inner wisdom.

Just remember: there's no one "right" way to experience a sound bath. It's all about letting go, surrendering to the sounds, and trusting the process.

1| You can join a local guided sound bath meditation or create your own cozy vibe at home using singing bowls, chimes, tuning forks, or even nature sounds. You can also find many recorded gong baths online.

2| When you're ready to begin, get comfy, whether you're lying down or sitting in a supported position. Close your eyes and let the sounds wash over you like a warm, soothing wave.

3| Focus on your breath, letting it deepen and slow down. As you listen, allow thoughts and worries to drift away like clouds in the sky.

4| Notice how the sounds resonate within your body. Do you feel a tingling? A sense of release? Pay attention to any shifts in your physical or emotional state. Be open to any insights or messages that might bubble up.

AFFIRMATIONS FOR ATTRACTING SPIRITUAL GROWTH

I am a masterpiece in progress, constantly evolving and blossoming.

My inner compass guides me with an unwavering certainty.

I radiate an aura of calm strength and self-belief.

I embrace vulnerability as an opportunity for deeper connection and authentic expression.

I honor my journey, celebrating both triumphs and setbacks as valuable lessons.

My voice is powerful and impactful, deserving to be heard.

I am a powerful creator of my own reality, manifesting my dreams with effortless grace.

I step into every situation with poise and an open heart.

I am a beacon of inspiration, illuminating my own path and that of others.

I am a masterpiece of resilience, gracefully navigating life's twists and turns.

My confidence is a vibrant flame, burning brightly within me.

I am limitless, capable of achieving anything I set my mind to.

Manifest Inner Peace and Happiness

In a world that often feels chaotic and overwhelming, finding inner peace and happiness can feel like a challenge. But it's possible! It's about learning to create a sense of calm within.

Manifesting peace and happiness isn't about ignoring problems or pretending everything's perfect; it's about building resilience and a positive mindset so you can handle life's ups and downs.

The exercises in this section will help you tap into your inner peace, let go of negativity and stress, and cultivate a life that feels truly joyful and fulfilling.

MANIFESTING MY PEACE

For a few years, I was trapped in a cycle of unhealthy behaviors, and unhealthy habits. I felt like a puppet on strings, controlled by forces beyond my grasp. I longed for freedom, for a way to break free from these patterns and reclaim my life. Then I realized I wasn't powerless, but a powerful creator with the ability to shape my reality.

I began exploring mindfulness, meditation, and manifestation, determined to heal and transform. Meditation was my first step. My mind resisted the stillness, craving the familiar

chaos, but gradually, I found moments of peace. I learned how to observe my cravings without giving in to them, and how to acknowledge my emotions without being consumed by them.

I started using affirmations, repeating empowering statements about my strength and resilience. I visualized my ideal self, free from these unhealthy patterns, radiating health and vitality. I focused on gratitude, appreciating the small joys and hope for a brighter future. The journey wasn't easy. There were days when temptation was overwhelming, pulling me back towards familiar patterns. But each time I stumbled, I found the strength to rise again, fueled by a growing belief in my own power to heal. Slowly, things shifted. The cravings lost their grip, replaced by a growing sense of self-worth and inner peace. I felt a surge of desire to create a life aligned with my true values.

Today, I'm living proof that we can break free from anything, even deeply ingrained patterns that hold us back.

THE INNER CHILD PLAYDATE

Tapping into your inner child is like hitting the reset button on being an adult. It's about reconnecting with that playful, curious, and joyful part of yourself that often gets buried under responsibilities and stress.

Play is a natural way to destress, unleash your creativity, and have some good old-fashioned fun. By embracing your inner child in this exercise, you're boosting your overall well-being. So give yourself permission to play—your soul will thank you.

1| Schedule dedicated time in your calendar for a playdate with your inner child. It could be an hour, an afternoon, or even a whole day.

2| Think back to the activities that lit you up as a kid. What did you love to do? Did you build epic creations, spend hours drawing, or explore the woods? Make a list of those activities and choose a few to revisit.

3| Now, dive into your chosen activities with abandon. Let go of any self-consciousness or worries about being productive. Embrace the freedom to be silly, creative, and fully present in the moment.

4| As you play, focus on the sensations in your body and the emotions you're experiencing. Notice the joy, excitement, and sense of wonder that bubbles up. Let go of any thoughts about the past or future and simply be here now.

THE ACTS OF KINDNESS CHALLENGE

Kindness is like a ripple in a pond, spreading outward and touching countless lives. This challenge is all about spreading kindness and watching the effect this positive energy has on you and others.

It's not about grand gestures; it's about those small, everyday acts that brighten someone's day and make your heart feel full.

Remember, even the smallest acts of kindness can make a huge difference, and you might be surprised at the sense of joy and fulfillment that comes from giving back.

1| Make a promise to yourself to perform at least one act of kindness every day. It doesn't have to be anything huge—even small gestures can make a big difference. Here are some ideas to get you started:

✦ Help a stranger carry their groceries.
✦ Pay for the person behind you in line at the coffee shop.
✦ Leave a kind note for your roommate or partner.
✦ Compliment a friend on their outfit or their work.
✦ Volunteer your time at a local charity or organization.
✦ Donate to a cause you care about.
✦ Simply smile at someone and offer a warm greeting.

2| Pay attention to how your acts of kindness impact others. Notice the smiles, the gratitude, and the positive energy you create.

THE INNER OASIS VISUALIZATION

Need a quick escape from the chaos of everyday life? This visualization exercise is your ticket to creating an inner sanctuary of peace and joy that you can access anytime, anywhere. It's like having a personal retreat center right inside your mind, ready to bring you back to center whenever you need it.

Think of this visualization as a mental reset. The more you practice, the easier it becomes to tap into those feelings of peace and happiness. This not only helps you chill out and reduce stress, but it also rewires your brain to associate those good vibes with your inner self.

1| Find a comfortable and quiet space where you won't be disturbed. Close your eyes and take a few deep breaths, allowing your body to relax and your mind to quiet down.

2| Now, picture a place that represents ultimate peace and happiness for you. It could be a secluded beach with turquoise waters, a sun-dappled forest clearing, a cozy cabin nestled in the mountains, or any other place that makes your soul smile.

3| Bring this mental image to life with vivid details:

- ✦ What do you see? Imagine the colors, textures, and landscapes that surround you.
- ✦ What do you hear? Is it the sound of waves crashing, birds chirping, or a gentle breeze rustling through the trees?
- ✦ What do you smell? The salty ocean air, the scent of pine needles, or maybe the aroma of freshly baked bread?

✦ What do you feel? The warmth of the sun on your skin, a cool breeze on your face, or the soft earth beneath your feet?

4| Imagine yourself fully immersed in this oasis. Feel the peace and happiness wash over you, melting away any worries or anxieties. Let go and simply bask in the tranquility of this moment.

5| As you experience this deep sense of peace and happiness, choose a simple gesture or word to anchor it in your memory. It could be a hand gesture, a word like "calm" or "bliss," or even a mental snapshot of your oasis.

6| Whenever you feel stressed, overwhelmed, or just need a mental break, close your eyes, take a deep breath, and revisit your inner oasis. Recall the sights, sounds, smells, and feelings you experienced. Use your anchor to quickly access this state of peace and joy.

AFFIRMATIONS FOR ATTRACTING INNER PEACE AND HAPPINESS

I am at peace with myself and the world around me.

I am filled with a deep sense of joy and contentment.

I radiate inner peace and serenity.

I am grateful for all the good in my life.

I am attracting positive experiences and relationships.

I am releasing all negativity and embracing peace.

I am creating a life filled with joy and happiness.

I am surrounded by love and support.

I am choosing peace and happiness in every moment.

I am worthy of a life filled with joy and contentment.

I am letting go of worry and embracing serenity.

I am finding peace within myself.

I am attracting abundance and happiness into my life.

I am living in alignment with my true self.

I am creating a life I love.

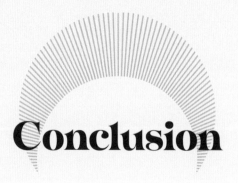

Conclusion

The journey of manifestation doesn't end with the final page of this book. It's an ongoing adventure, a lifelong dance with the universe. I urge you to embrace these tools and practices and to make them a part of your everyday life. Go forth and create the life you've always dreamed of; the world is waiting for your magic to shine.

If you've ever doubted your ability to create the life you desire, let this book be a reminder that you hold the keys to your own destiny. The universe is abundant, and there is more than enough for everyone. By aligning with your authentic self and embracing the power of manifestation, you can unlock a world of limitless possibilities.

Writing this book has been more than just a creative endeavor for me; it's been a profound personal transformation. As I poured my heart and soul onto these pages, I found myself embodying the very principles I was sharing. I witnessed my own dreams taking shape, my own life blossoming with abundance and joy.

It's my deepest hope that these words have not only informed you but also ignited a spark of possibility within you, a belief that you, too, can create a life beyond your wildest dreams.

You are not alone. The universe is cheering you on, and so am I. Embrace the journey, celebrate your each of your victories, and learn from your challenges.

Every step you take, no matter how small, is a step toward the life you envision. The power to manifest your dreams is within you.

Now, go forth and unleash it!

About the Author

Nicole Weiss is a manifestation mentor, full-time creator, and published author. Her journey started as a tattoo artist, where she honed her creative skills and passion for self-expression. Now, as a busy mom of three in the mountains of Utah, she empowers others to design their dream lives through the power of manifestation.

With over 13 years of experience, she brings a wealth of knowledge to her work, guiding individuals to manifest their dreams. She believes that everyone holds the power to create their dream reality, and through her writing and online presence, she empowers people to overcome limiting beliefs and manifest a life aligned with their soul's purpose.

Find Nicole on Youtube, Instagram, and Tiktok @Manifex for more manifesting magic and inspiration!

About the Illustrator

Annie Tarasova is an artist on a mission to inspire you to look within, as she believes all answers can be found in your inner world.

Based in Australia, she runs her own business DreamyMoons, designing guided journals and card decks to inspire personal growth and mindfulness. Her biggest passion is connecting others to their imagination and creative powers.

Find Annie on Instagram @dreamy_moons.

Recommended Reading

The World Is a Mirror,
Nada Amari

Becoming Supernatural,
Dr. Joe Dispenza

*Breaking the Habit of
Being Yourself,*
Dr. Joe Dispenza

The Power of Intention,
Wayne Dyer

Ask and It Is Given,
Esther and Jerry Hicks

A New Earth,
Eckhart Tolle

Index

A

abundance
- abundance check exercise 156–7
- affirmations for attracting 162–3
- gratitude jar for abundance 130–1
- manifesting money and abundance 152–63

affirmations 14, 79
- attracting career success 172–3
- attracting confidence and self-esteem 200–1, 208–9
- attracting health and wellness 182–3
- attracting inner peace and happiness 214–15
- attracting love 150–1
- attracting money and abundance 162–3
- break free from self-doubt 57
- find your inner power 81
- inner champion affirmation mirror ritual 196
- inspired action 109
- positive mindset affirmation ritual 50–1
- trust the universe 135
- unveil your wishes 37

B

beliefs
- limiting 38
- replacing self-limiting 14, 40–59
- self-belief 194

C

careers 30
- act as if method 168–9
- affirmations for attracting career success 172–3
- manifestation roadmap for a dream job 92–3

childhood
- inner child playdate 210
- compassion, self- 48
- confidence 148, 149
- breaking free from self-doubt 14, 40–59
- confidence-boosting visualization 197–8

D

decluttering method 160–1
doubt, self- 38, 192
- breaking free from 14, 40–59
- daily affirmations to break free from 57
- facing your self-doubt exercise 46–7
- journal prompts to break free from 56

dreams
- believing in 83
- decoding dreams 106–7
- designing your dream day 34–5
- dream life vision board 32–3
- shower ritual to manifest your dreams 78–9

E

emotions 79
- embracing 77
- emotional well-being 31

F

family 29
- family gratitude practices 129
food
- mindful grocery shopping exercise 181
- recipe adventure 180
forgiveness 127

G

gratitude 17, 120–1, 202
- body gratitude ritual 178–9
- grateful money manifestation 152–3
- gratitude jar for abundance 130–1
- gratitude letter to the universe 132–3
- short daily gratitude practice 128–9

H

happiness
- affirmations for attracting 216
health 29, 174–83
- affirmations for attracting 182–3
- healthy habits ritual 176–7

I

imposter syndrome 44
inner champion affirmation mirror ritual 196
inner child 123
- inner child playdate 212
- the inner child reconnection 189
inner critic
- challenging your 48–9
- inner oasis visualization 214–15
inner peace 31, 119, 202
- affirmations for attracting 216
- manifesting 210–17
inspired action
- act as if method 168–9
- inspired action dare 98–9
- inspired action reward system 100–1
intuition 110

J

jobs
- manifestation roadmap for dream 92–3
journaling
- connecting with your true self 71
- dig up your dreams journaling exercise 24
- journal prompts to break free from self-doubt 56

journal prompts to find your inner power 80
journal prompts to take inspired action 108–9
journal prompts to trust the universe 134
journal prompts to unveil your wishes 36
living the dream journal 170–1
soul's calling journaling exercise, the 186–7

K
kindness 47
    acts of kindness challenge 213

L
Law of Assumption 64–5, 68–9, 82
Law of Attraction 15, 63, 64–5, 66–7, 82, 120
Law of Detachment 110–11, 118–19, 121
letting go 127
    burning bowl release ritual 126–7
    letting go of possessions 160
    release attachment meditation ritual 124–5
life
    dream life vision board 32–3
    living the dream journal 170–1
love
    affirmations for attracting love 150–151
    future love time capsule manifestation 146–7
    love letter method, the 144
    manifesting love and self-love 142–51
    mirror work for love method 149
    self-love date ritual 148
    whisper method, the 145

M
meditations 55
    connecting with your true self 71
    guided meditation to meet your future self 74–5
    meditation to clear mental clutter 52–3
    money magnet meditation 158–9
    purposeful pause meditation, the 190–1
    release attachment meditation ritual 124–5
mindfulness
    connecting with your true self 71
    mindful grocery shopping exercise, the 181
    mindful movement ritual 177
mirror work 76–7
    mirror work for love method 149
money
    369 money manifesting exercise 154–5
    grateful money manifestation 152–3
    money magnet meditation 158–9
morning hydration ritual 177
movement ritual, mindful 177

N
negativity 174
    breaking free from self-doubt 14, 40–59

P
pause meditation, the purposeful 190–1
peace, inner 119, 202, 210–17
purpose 31
    purposeful pause meditation, the 190–1
    purposeful playlist creation, the 188

R
release
    burning bowl release ritual 126–7
    release attachment meditation ritual 124–5
    release and flow water ritual 122–3
reward systems, inspired action 100–1

S
sacred space creation 205
self, the
    aligning with your authentic self visualization 70–1
    guided meditation to meet your future self 74–5
soul, the
    soul-nourishing activities list 204
    soul's calling journaling exercise, the 186–7
symbolic animals 103

T
time capsule manifestation, future love 146–7

U
universe, the
    communicating with the 105
    cosmic scavenger hunt 104–5
    gratitude letter to the universe 132–3
    signs from the 16, 87, 103
    trusting the 17, 112–37
    "universe, show me a sign" challenge, the 102–3

V
vision boards, dream life 32–3
visualizations 15, 79
    aligning with your authentic self visualization 70–1
    confidence-boosting visualization 198–9
    inner oasis visualization 214–15

W
whisper method, the 145
wishes
    creating your wish list 26–7, 28–31

Acknowledgments

To my incredible husband, thank you for showing me that anything I want to do can truly be my reality. None of this would've been possible without you.

To my precious children, you can be whoever you want to be. The world is yours to explore and create.

To my loving mom and dad, thank you for always believing in me, no matter what I pursued.

To my amazing sister, there are simply not enough words to express how deeply you've inspired me throughout my life. I love and admire you beyond measure.